B UILDING THE COLLECTIVE

BUILDING THE COLLECTIVE
SOVIET GRAPHIC DESIGN 1917–1937
SELECTIONS FROM THE MERRILL C. BERMAN COLLECTION

LEAH DICKERMAN, EDITOR

PRINCETON ARCHITECTURAL PRESS

Published by
Princeton Architectural Press
37 East 7th Street New York, NY 10003
(212) 995-9620

In association with an exhibition held at
the Miriam and Ira D. Wallach Art Gallery,
Columbia University

ISBN 1-56898-074-4 paper

Printed and bound in Canada
Design by Allison Saltzman
Photography by Jim Frank

Library of Congress cataloging-in-publication data
Building the collective : Soviet graphic design, 1917–1937 :
selections from the Merrill C. Berman collection /
edited by Leah Dickerman.
p. cm.
Includes bibliographical references.
ISBN 1-56898-074-4 (pbk. : alk. paper)
1. Political posters, Russian.
2. Soviet Union—History—1917–1936—Posters.
3. Berman, Merrill C.
I. Dickerman, Leah, 1964–   .
DK266.B844   1996
741.6'7'094709041—dc20   95–51211
CIP

For a free catalog of other books published by Princeton Architectural Press,
call toll free (800) 722-6657

Visit Princeton Architectural Press on the web at http://www.designsys.com/pap

Contents

Building the Collective

FOREWORD

Conceived and organized by Leah Dickerman, an advanced graduate student in Columbia University's Department of Art History and Archaeology, *Building the Collective* stems from her doctoral dissertation on the work of the Soviet artist Aleksandr Rodchenko. During the course of Ms. Dickerman's research on Rodchenko, she had the opportunity to examine one of the most significant collections of graphic design anywhere in the world—that of Merrill C. Berman. The idea for the current exhibition grew out of this meeting between a scholar and a collector, and the Miriam and Ira D. Wallach Art Gallery is honored to be mounting such a large selection of important works from the Berman collection. One of the most comprehensive groups of Soviet posters and graphic works to be shown in the United States, this exhibition explores the ways in which graphic design was used to address and to construct a collective audience. Without the enthusiasm and commitment of Ms. Dickerman and Mr. Berman, the project could not have been possible. All of us connected with the Wallach Art Gallery are particularly grateful to Mr. Berman for his unfailing goodwill, cooperation, and enormous reservoir of expertise at all points during the organization of the exhibition.

The Wallach Art Gallery was created with the intention that many of its exhibitions would be the outgrowth of research by graduate students and faculty in the art history department, and *Building the Collective* admirably fulfills that aim. Its realization has been due to the efforts and generosity of many people. Special thanks go to Professor Johanna Drucker of Yale University for her guidance and assistance; to Maria Gough for her essay contribution to the catalog; to Jim Frank for color photography; to Kevin Lippert and Allison Saltzman of Princeton Architectural Press; and to two anonymous donors whose support allowed the exhibition to take place.

Jonathan Crary
Associate Professor of Art History, Columbia University
Chair, Miriam and Ira D. Wallach Art Gallery Steering Committee

BUILDING THE COLLECTIVE

LEAH DICKERMAN

When the Bolsheviks seized power in October 1917 in the name of the proletariat, they did so with the promise of a socialist future as a technologically advanced collective society; they pledged, that is, both radical democratization and rapid industrialization. For the first time in history, a secular government defined an overarching world-view—a theorized stance from which to interpret and transform society.[1] Labor, technology, and industrialization were seen, along with political revolution, as the means to produce a new political subject, one capable of perceiving and acting upon its class interests in a collective way. Nowhere was this aspiration towards the collective more clearly delineated than in the early Soviet poster. In the Soviet Union, graphic design became a highly developed and far-reaching political medium; it not only addressed a mass audience, but represented it and strove to shape it, working to transform the laboring masses into a politically aware, unified, and productive class. Through its instrumental, public function, graphic work also served as a field in which many artists attempted to redefine their own role within the new society.

"Free working hands of the collective farms, to industry!," a photomontage poster made during the industrialization drive of the First Five-Year Plan (1928–32), signals some of the broad themes of this exhibition. (no. 89) On the left side, defined by a bright orange band, an amorphous crowd gathers. Moving rightward is

89

a well-ordered line of workers atop a factory complex, built in the steel and glass idiom of industrial modernism. Each is equipped, ready to labor, and progressively larger than the worker behind. A large-scale, disembodied hand, positioned at the intersection of these two images, inscribes the word "Contract" in careful script. Suggesting the individual's conscious recognition and acceptance of communal goals, the writing hand stands as the way-station in the transformation of the unruly masses into an organized, revolutionary collective. Bound by labor, industrialization, and technology, the collective is the most consistent, even defining, trope of the Soviet Union. *Building the Collective* examines its manifestations and transformations in the graphic arts during the first, crucial decades after the founding of the Soviet state—from the Civil War through the Second Five-Year Plan.

Just after the February 1917 revolution, which had deposed the Tsar, there were other alternatives, other utopian visions trumpeted from the left; the Socialist Revolutionary party, for example, promoted a radical agrarian socialism that appealed strongly to the largely disenfranchised rural population. But in seizing power on the night of October 24th–25th, the Bolsheviks preempted any popular preference for this pastoral vision of the world to come. It was a coup in the name not only of the working class, but also of an industrialized future.

World War I had provided the Bolshevik leaders with a crucial lesson regarding the importance of technology, as Vladimir Lenin wrote in 1918 at the time of signing the treaty in Brest-Litovsk, ending Russia's participation in that conflict:

> The war has taught us much; not only that people suffered, but especially the fact that those who have the best technology, organization, and best machines emerge on top. It is essential to learn that without machines, without discipline, it is impossible to live in modern society. It is necessary to master the highest technology or be crushed.[2]

But at the same time, the mechanized death of war pushed into the foreground the ruinous potential of technology. The social and cultural commentator Walter Benjamin understood the Russian Revolution against this traumatic background, calling it the "first attempt of mankind to bring the new body [of technology] under control."[3] Artists of the Russian avant-garde also felt the imperative to reclaim the progressive potential of technology, which had been diverted, in El Lissitzky's words, "from the path of construction to the path of death and destruction."[4]

With the Bolsheviks in power, the October dream of an industrial, technological utopia immediately confronted unavoidable questions: Could labor in Soviet Russia be qualitatively different from the oppressive and alienating labor of capitalist societies described by Karl Marx? Could technology be harnessed to progressive purpose? Leon Trotskii recognized the paradox posed by technology, understanding it as both an alienating force and potentially liberating one, but nonetheless maintained optimism about its promise. In 1926, he wrote:

[Technology] has...served up to the present as an instrument for exploitation; yet, it is, at the same time, the fundamental condition for the emancipation of the exploited. The machine strangles the wage-slave in its grip. But he can free himself only through the machine.[5]

Bolshevik leaders, such as Trotskii, firmly believed that the transformation of class relations through political revolution—through the acquisition of the means of production—would eliminate the threat of alienation posed to the working class by technology.

In early Soviet Russia, a certain semantic and ideological slippage existed in the terms "industrialization" and "revolution." The common phrases "socialist construction" and "building socialism" referred simultaneously to the creation of an industrial base and to the production of a collective consciousness as a kind of social superstructure. Technology was seen not only to provide the means to an economic surplus, but, like revolution, to create a new kind of political entity. Lenin described electrification in the hands of the proletarian state, for example, as the catalyst to "the final victory of the foundation of a civilized life without exploiters, without capitalists, without landowners, without merchants."[6] Such a concept was also embodied in the Bolshevik leader's famous slogan, ubiquitous even until the collapse of the Soviet Union (and appearing in this exhibition in one of Gustav Klutsis's posters [no. 59]): "COMMUNISM EQUALS SOVIET POWER PLUS ELECTRIFICATION." Trotskii went further, implying that Communism could be defined as the technological structuring of humankind. "Socialist construction," he wrote, was "an attempt to rationalize human relationships, i.e., to subordinate them to reason armed with science."[7]

Beyond emphasizing the transformative powers of technology, the Soviets understood—better than their political rivals—that mass politics required mass communication. Lenin asserted, in one of his blunt formulations, that "Socialism without a postal and telegraph service is the emptiest of phrases."[8] The recognition of a gap between psychological attitudes and the fact of revolution made the creation of a new socialist subject a political imperative. The Bolsheviks turned to propaganda to narrow this gulf. The immediate aim of Soviet publicity was to cultivate support for the Bolshevik regime and their demands, and the new government raised mass communication to the level of a policy issue, dedicating several agencies to political education. Yet beyond specific pragmatic goals, the early Soviet government initiated many efforts at developing informed participation—efforts which cannot be understood simply in terms of a cynical political instrumentality. In the program of its Eighth Congress in 1919, the Party committed itself to developing a "continually rising standard of culture, organization, and self-activity on the part of the masses."[9] Mass communication was an important tool in the attempt to transform the working-class population into a politically and technologically conscious collective.

Posters came to occupy a central role in this concerted effort to build broad-reaching information technologies, to develop systems of mass communication which would bind and influence their audience. Effective in reaching a largely illiterate population and—because of their address of a mass, rather than individual, readership—relatively frugal in their use of materials in short supply, posters were among the first means of mass propagation to be developed. The announcement of the Party organ *Pravda* on October 6, 1918 that "the poster must become a new, powerful weapon of socialist propaganda, with the objective of influencing the broadest masses" noted the poster's particular ability to attract the attention of the distracted crowd, creating "a first impression on their consciousness which lectures and books can subsequently deepen."[10] Yet even well after literacy rates rose and the shortages of civil war eased, posters and other forms of graphic design continued to be a significant element of the Soviet government's communication arsenal, certainly because posters remain among the most potent means to infuse public space with ideological messages.

Posters also took on a central ideological significance in artists' efforts to redefine their own role within Soviet society. As an inherently public medium, openly instrumental and mass-reproduced, posters exist at a great remove from the realm of high art. For many avant-garde artists whose work is shown in this exhibition, including Gustav Klutsis, El Lissitzky, and Aleksandr Rodchenko, poster production was at once state-sponsored propaganda *and* self-conscious critique of the traditional art object, an announcement of art's irrelevance to the new society; for these artists, work in the field of poster design stood as a disavowal both of the unique and eternal work hung in a ritual exhibition space and of the hermetic self-reflexivity of high modernism. "With our work," wrote Lissitzky, "the Revolution has achieved a colossal labor of propaganda and enlightenment. We ripped up the traditional book into single posters in the streets....The innovation of easel painting made great works of art possible but it has now lost its power."[11] Other more traditional artists, such as Aleksandr Deineka and Aleksandr Samokhvalov, continued to create easel paintings alongside their poster production; for them the poster served as an alternative canvas. In addition, some of the images in the exhibition were produced by graphic designers and political cartoonists, such as Aleksei Radakov and Viktor Deni, who worked in the mass media even before the Revolution and for whom the issue of high art simply did not arise. Many of the conceptual and aesthetic differences between works can be attributed to these distinctions. In the Civil War period, for example, poster production encompassed works that adapted popular graphic traditions and colloquial speech patterns to address the proletariat on what was seen as its own terms, as well as works that attempted the difficult task of making the visual language of modernism politically effective, yoking the geometric abstraction of Suprematism to didactic text. And later, there was an increasing divergence between the Constructivist mandate to produce an image requiring an active labor of interpretation on the part of the viewer, on the one hand, and iconic representations of heroic workers soliciting the viewer's identification on the other.

Yet it is important to emphasize that *all* the artists and designers who produced posters for Soviet agencies were united by their commitment to convey a message, producing images of a certain basic readability—a mandate which was not without its ideological tensions and aesthetic contradictions. Moreover, as the designers were not, for the most part, from working-class backgrounds, the posters can also be seen as an attempt on the part of artists to negotiate between themselves, bourgeois professionals in the service of the new regime, and the audience of workers they addressed.

Within the diversity of practice seen in the exhibition, the construction of images of labor and the proletarian collective roughly correspond to periods of dramatic historical change. An insistent effort to define a proletarian identity for the new state and to interpret contemporary events through the lens of class struggle characterized the graphic work of the Civil War period (1918–21), while during the limited market economy of the New Economic Policy (1921–27), artists strove to distinguish Soviet labor and its products from those of capitalism. The technification and militarization of the image of the collective accompanied the radical questioning of traditional social and cultural values of the First Five-Year Plan (1928–32; it was completed in four years). And a newly corporeal and hierarchical representation of labor, defined through the monumental figures of the exemplary worker-hero and the great leader, emerged in the years of the Second Five-Year Plan (1933–37).

Though it is to some extent true for all works of art, the sale, collection, exhibition, and reproduction for publication of Soviet graphic design of the immediately post-revolutionary period presents a particular dilemma for the art historian. The removal of these works from their original context and their re-inscription in a contemporary Western space makes it difficult to recover their historically specific purpose and their imbrication within the discussions and debates of a complex period. There is no way to fully overcome this. However, through its organization around a theme of particular historical relevance, its divisions into groupings that reflect aesthetic and ideological shifts, and its stacked installation—meant to evoke the postered wall rather than the modern museum—*Building the Collective* attempts to maintain a certain sensitivity to the historical gap that separates us from the works' original, graphically inscribed Soviet audience. (The very fact that the posters' slogans must often not only be translated, but also explained—and the act of attention demanded of the contemporary viewer—demonstrates the difficulty of such an enterprise.) What follows is an attempt to establish an overall time line, which will permit the viewer to situate specific images accordingly. One risks oversimplifying and broadly generalizing in the effort to excavate something of the historical meaning beneath the graphic surface. It is not the intention of this essay to establish a straightforwardly deterministic model, nor to claim that each poster is a direct reflection of a particular historical moment. But these works do address a particular audience in an attempt to respond to both general and specific political imperatives. Their relationship to history is dialogical, and they say as much about the self-definition of the artist as they do about the period. This essay's insistence on context, therefore, at once attempts to mute the object status that these works have accrued *and* to evoke the problematic of art-making in the early Soviet period; for it is precisely by virtue of its mass production and instrumental purpose that graphic design is not merely a by-product of Soviet artistic production, but the field in which the changing role of the artist comes out with the greatest clarity and force.

THE CIVIL WAR

Though the Bolsheviks seized power in October 1917, poster production did not begin in earnest until the middle of 1918. This date marked the start of the Civil War, when the new regime found itself challenged by a variety of anti-Bolshevik forces, both foreign and domestic—the latter called Whites in contrast to the Soviet, or Red, Army. Then, the flood-gates of propaganda opened: in his book on the early Bolshevik poster, Stephen White estimates that approximately 4,000 political posters were issued between 1918 and 1921.[12] Many Civil War posters were produced by the Red Army's propaganda arm, the Political Directorate of the Revolutionary Military Council of RSFSR or Revvoensovet, which was under the ultimate direction of Trotskii. The significance of the poster-making enterprise as part of the war effort was signaled by the autonomy, technical assistance, and privileged access to supplies granted to it by the government.

The central importance of posters becomes especially clear when their production is situated against a background of severe material and labor shortages. Qualified printers and press-workers were often lost to conscription or through their hostility to the Bolsheviks. The Baltic region, with most of the paper-making factories, was occupied, and supplies of spare parts for foreign-made printing presses were cut off by battle lines and economic embargoes.[13] In an effort to ease the situation, the Soviet government claimed a monopoly on what paper supplies there were, and all paper not distributed by the government was subject to confiscation.[14]

Moreover, poster-making during the Civil War was not a commitment lightly made: more was at stake than the identity of the commissioning agency. Viacheslav Polonskii, in charge of poster-publishing for the Red Army, noted that the number of artists willing to work for him declined precipitously when Denikin's White Army advanced towards Tula in the summer of 1919.[15] One put one's life on the line with the act of postering for either side; many of the early posters produced by Revvoensovet bear the ominous warning: "Anyone tearing down this poster or pasting over it commits a counter-revolutionary act." (see no. 1, no. 12)

Thus, the first Bolshevik posters should be read against the cacophony of the Civil War as they attempted to elicit support for a regime that was in fierce competition with other, stridently anti-Communist voices also claiming political authority. Using the rhetoric of class struggle, Bolshevik posters exhorted the population to provide fighting men, labor, goods, and the tacit support necessary to conduct war—

and conversely to withhold such assistance from the Whites. But more than just a set of material and logistical demands, these posters were the beginning of the Soviet attempt to present and create a specifically proletarian identity. As historian Sheila Fitzpatrick notes, the Bolsheviks insistently portrayed the struggle in class terms at both a domestic and an international level—the Russian proletariat against the Russian bourgeoisie; Soviet Communism against oppressive, international Capitalism.[16] The early Soviet government claimed to rule as a class-based collective—the so-called "dictatorship of the proletariat"—and embraced the coercion and destruction of other classes that this implied. Calling for "the ruthless suppression of the exploiters," the July 1918 Constitution of the Russian Socialist Soviet Republic [RSFSR] most explicitly did *not* grant equal rights to all, but rather established a complex system of class-discriminatory laws, disenfranchised members of the former privileged classes, and weighted urban workers' votes heavily in relation to those of the peasantry.[17] It mattered very much who ruled whom. Vengeance, rightful inheritance, the need for vigilance against class enemies, and celebration of the reversal of power relations were all common themes in the posters of the Civil War. Distancing themselves from what they saw as the genteel hypocrisy of the bourgeoisie, the Communists displayed a certain pride in tough talk, and their posters, in both text and image, were rich in the depiction of violence.

The revolution was often presented as a moment of wholesale rupture—the line dividing "before" from "after." An early image signed "S.A.," for example, cuts the visual field in two. (no. 5) On the left, a worker is shown in the middle distance carefully applying oil to the wheels of a giant green locomotive. Below the caption reads: "Earlier I was an oiler, I oiled the wheels." In the right-hand panel, the same worker, identified by his checked pants, jumps to the foreground. There, in a columned, red-walled room and in front of an attentive audience, he gestures with oratorical drama. The caption underscores the transformation of working man into power-holder. "And now," it reads, "I'm in the Soviet. I decide issues." With the revolution, the poster asserts, class relations have been entirely inverted.

Above all, the Civil War era posters begin to define the boundaries—both from the inside and from the outside—of the new, proletarian ruling class. In Dmitrii Moor's 1919 poster "Everyone to the defense," the red Communist star appears above a crenelated fortress wall. (no. 1) In the center, a worker, a peasant, and a Communist study a battle map; the last calls in strategic orders over a telephone. A golden halo emanates from the attenuated arms of electric lamps extending out from behind this modern trinity, while the threatening figures of "Hunger" and "Slavery" lurk in the upper corners, dressed in their elegant bourgeois garb. Five social groups inhabit the interstices of the star's pointed arms, each functioning in relation to the others. The Communist "points out the enemy and leads into battle"; the peasant feeds the fighters; the woman takes over for the man away at the front; the youth train in order to carry the torch; and the worker forges weapons. Together they form the fighting collective of the revolutionary proletariat, united by technology and a common struggle with the capitalist world.

5

1

The proletariat was understood by the Soviets as a class entity extending beyond Russia's borders and encompassing all workers of the world, bound together in fraternal solidarity. Groups who had lost their cultural autonomy under Tsarist rule were supposed to embrace the Moscow government in an alliance of the formerly oppressed. In another poster by Moor, members of various Caucasian ethnic minorities greet, with open arms, a Communist on horseback gesturing his benevolent recognition. (no. 6) Clearly the image reflects ideological expectation far more than the reality of the welcome.

In a pattern that was to be repeated during the First Five-Year Plan, the definition of the proletariat in Civil War posters is as much a matter of exclusion as inclusion. The class enemy is portrayed in a poster by Viktor Deni. Beneath the flag of the White General Denikin (which bears the inscription "Beat the workers and the peasants") the artist groups Denikin himself, a reactionary member of the Duma, a capitalist, a priest, a wealthy peasant or *kulak*, a White officer, and a drunken White infantryman in an alliance of greed and villainy. (no. 11)

As the caricatures in the Deni poster suggest, in the contentious atmosphere of the Civil War, satire was a primary weapon. Its importance reflects both the exigencies of the era—the need to tar the enemy with the widest and blackest possible brush—as well as the journalistic background of the designers who were the first to identify themselves with the new regime. Artists such as Moor, Deni, and Aleksei Radakov were not painters from a high-art background; rather, they had long produced socially engaged work, having served before the Revolution as cartoonists and illustrators for newspapers and journals. For an artist like Moor, who had run an underground press and contributed satirical cartoons to a series of semi-legal journals in the period immediately following the 1905 Revolution, identification with the Soviet government was the culmination of a long journey out from the underground.[18]

Of all the early Bolshevik poster artists, Deni remained closest to the tradition of satirical graphics, and his work often appears as an enlarged form of the journal page. But turning wit to social purpose, almost all of the Civil War period poster designers made use of the graphic devices and tropes of political cartoons, such as before-and-after schema, carnivalesque inversions of expected hierarchies, and a cast of easily recognizable stock caricatures. True to the satiric tradition, the grotesque is often used to delineate and reinforce the boundaries of the proletariat, and class enemies appear as monsters and monstrosities. In a work by Deni, a distorted and distended bourgeois in a black suit and jewels cowers beneath the words "Third International"—the meeting of international Communist organizations to promote world revolution—inscribed by a menacing red hand. (no. 14) A bright yellow banner within another poster by Deni is inscribed "Capitalists of all nations unite!" in a satiric transformation of the Communist motto. (no. 12) Below the banner, Deni pictures this "collective" with scorching irony: the bloated figures of France, the United States, and England, their bodies formed by money bags, blow smoke rings from cigars clenched between their teeth. Gallows stand behind them and the

6

11

contorted bodies of workers lie below. (Deni's capitalist figures, however, are no match for the taut muscularity of Moor's red-shirted Saturday laborers in his "First of May" poster. [no. 10]) In the "Third International" poster, satire functions as a kind of unmasking, presenting the "true" class relations that structure historical experience. Insisting on its historical specificity and pointing emphatically outside the work to the world beyond, its reading requires a kind of decoding, a movement of comparison and interpretation back and forth between the art object and the social world.

12

With its quickly changing conditions, the Civil War provided the crucible in which Soviet systems of mass communication were formed. In one of the most remarkable early Soviet innovations in communication technology, poster-making was enlisted to respond to and comment on current events as they unfolded. Using the telegraph to relay information to artists producing posters, the Russian Telegraph Agency [ROSTA] inaugurated a virtual broadcast medium aimed at a mass audience over great distance—a primitive paper precursor to the introduction of radio.[19] Not only were the posters intended for a broad audience, but the process of design and production was itself a collaborative enterprise, employing over 100 people at its height in 1920.[20] While the identity of the artists who worked within the ROSTA group—including Mikhail Cheremnykh, Ivan Maliutin, and the poet Vladimir Maiakovskii—has been well documented by later Soviet art historians, all the posters were in fact unsigned.

News or information that determined the basic theme of each poster came in over the telegraph system or was culled from the Party press by Maiakovskii. A text was quickly formulated, and an artist associated with the ROSTA cooperative created a corresponding set of images. Different teams of workers then made copies from the stencils.[21] (These were used not only because of a shortage of printing presses, but also because the process of generation was quicker than producing a lithographic plate.) Individual images were generally reproduced between 50 and 200 times, as Maiakovskii later recalled.[22]

10

Above all, production was quick; posters were generally hung the morning after a report was transmitted or a decree was published, and in certain circumstances they were up in less than an hour—a speed of production that allowed for tremendous responsiveness to the political and logistical exigencies of the day.[23] They were pasted up in well-trafficked public areas, occasionally in empty show windows (as their common name of *okna ROSTA* or "ROSTA windows" suggests), but more often on kiosks, in stations, and around markets, to be read collectively and publicly. Maiakovskii described the ROSTA posters as "telegraphic bulletins, instantly translated into poster form, decrees immediately published as rhymes. The vulgar character of the poetry, the coarse character—this is due not only to the absence of paper, but also to the furious tempo of the revolution with which printing technology could not keep pace."[24]

The ROSTA posters attempted in both text and image to develop a specifically proletarian voice—to address the audience as comrades. They drew on the vernacular genres of political cartoons and traditional Russian popular prints, called *lubki*, which combined illustrations and text and frequently satirized figures and events in an allegorical mode to produce condensed and readable images. The familiar "you" form was used to address the posters' intended proletarian audience, and the caption texts, which drew on working-class speech, were idiomatic and often crude, rhythmic, and punning, like the images themselves.

The use of such a colloquial voice to build communal, class-based solidarity is seen in the ROSTA poster series in this exhibition, designed by Ivan Maliutin. (The poster group [no. 16] is labelled GPP n. 392 because it was made after January 1921, when Glavpolitprosvet, a department of the Commissariat of the Enlightenment, assumed administration of the ROSTA poster-making collaborative.) In spare images evoking wood-block prints, Maliutin represents a world hostile or indifferent to Soviet Russia, even in the face of the mass starvation on the Volga. Images of purposeless waste resonate through repetition—the obesity of the Western representatives, their extended and futile negotiations, the tons of excess wheat rotting in Canada, and finally, the lives lost along the Volga. With the viscerally violent (and emphatically vernacular) summons "Fingers on the throat, knee in the gut!", a red-shirted worker (a common trope in the ROSTA posters, representing the socialist collective, the good politically conscious laborer, or good Communist forces in general) calls his proletarian comrades (and the viewer) to righteous vengeance in the name of the working class.

In attempting to extend the reach of the ROSTA network, posters (and some-times stencils as well) were sent from Moscow to provincial centers for reproduction. Maliutin wrote a handbook on the technique of stencil-making to be distributed to regional groups in order to facilitate local production.[25] With central encourage-ment, regional ROSTA offices were established, which quickly took on distinctive, local character and often made use of wholly different techniques. Two of these regional ROSTA groups, Petrograd and Smolensk, are represented by works in the show.

The Petrograd ROSTA collaborative was set up in April 1920 by the artists Vladimir Kozlinskii and Vladimir Lebedev, and produced more than 1000 posters in the span of two years.[26] Most of the Petrograd ROSTA posters were linocuts, avoid-ing the time-consuming technique of the lithographic plate and the need for press-es, as the Moscow group had with their use of stencils. The production process was overseen by Kozlinskii in the graphic workshops of the former Academy of Art, an appropriation of the Tsarist institution emphasizing the inversions of power wrought by the Revolution.

Even at this stage, considerable manipulations of the facts were required in order to construct an image of a cohesive collective united under the Communist Party. The starkness of the gap between representation and political reality comes out in one of the Petersburg images by Kozlinskii, captioned "The Kronstadt card is beaten!" (no. 20) At Kronstadt, sailors, who had been among those to participate in the October Revolution, rebelled, protesting the arbitrary rule of the Communist

Party and demanding a government of genuine worker-peasant representation. Party officials, Red Army troops, and internal security forces converged
on Kronstadt and, turning their guns on the sailors, suppressed the rebellion.
In what Fitzpatrick calls the first wholesale attempt in Soviet Russia to manipulate
the representation of current events through the mass media, the Party blamed
the Kronstadt revolt on a conspiracy led by White Guards and a foreign general,
thus denying by omission and displacement that this had been a revolt by *bona
fide* members of the revolutionary proletariat.[27] Challenging the primary equation
made between the Communist Party and workers' rule, Kronstadt posed a
threat aimed at the heart of the Soviet ideological enterprise. Kozlinskii's poster
participates in what was a general effort to mute its implications. Mimicking the
format of a playing card, the poster is marked by spades—the suit associated
with subterfuge and misfortune; within, an elegant set of maskings, unmaskings,
and inversions take place. The faceless figure of a White Guard appears in
the top half of the poster's frame, brandishing a cat-o'-nine tail—the whip a
symbol of his openly evil persona. Below, and joined to the White Guard in a
Janus-like configuration, is a trusty Soviet sailor, sporting striped ribbons and a
pert mustache. But things are not what they seem, for the sailor points with a
delicate finger to a small sign (which mirrors the position of the whip) bearing
the letters SR—indicating the Socialist Revolutionary Party, the Bolsheviks' rivals
for the loyalty of the laboring classes. Stamped in red across both figures is
RSFSR—the acronym for the Russian Socialist Federation of Soviet Russia—the
true voice of the proletariat. Mere appearances, the posters imply, are not
to be believed. (Of course, the supposed "true" reality underneath is itself a
construction of propaganda, a card trick from the stacked deck of Bolshevik
realpolitik.)

While the ROSTA posters dealt with immediate concerns, they also attempted
to situate both the revolution and the accompanying artistic enterprise against
a more distant historical backdrop. One Petersburg image by Kozlinskii, (no. 19)
with the text "The dead of the Paris Commune have risen under the red banner of
the Soviets," links the ROSTA project to an earlier tradition of revolutionary art-
making. Kozlinskii borrows the main figure on the barricade from Eugène Delacroix's
famous "Liberty Leading the People," made for the Salon of 1830, the year of
popular uprisings. (Here, Kozlinskii elides the Commune with this earlier revolution.)
Yet, Kozlinskii substitutes a bearded working-class fighter for the half-draped female
allegorical figure of Marianne in Delacroix's work. Rather than Delacroix's lush
painterly realism, he uses a fractured modernist idiom built of flat planes of color,
thus adapting the figure on the barricade for a modern moment; and, rather than a
unique painting, Kozlinskii produces a poster manufactured and issued in multiple
to be hung on public walls. The successful Soviet Revolution becomes the redemp-
tive fulfillment of the failed Commune, and the ROSTA project, the rightful heir to
Delacroix's revolutionary icon.

20

19

If Kozlinskii's image linked the poster-making enterprise with a distant artistic past, the artists of the ROSTA center in Smolensk were more concerned with integrating the more immediate avant-garde legacy into their political work. Smolensk ROSTA was closely connected to the Suprematist collective, UNOVIS [*utverditeli novogo iskusstva*, or Affirmers of the New Art], which had formed around the artist Kazimir Malevich at the Vitebsk State Free Art Workshops in 1919. Artists Wladyslaw Strzeminski and Katarzyna Kobro headed an art workshop in Smolensk which became a *de facto* branch of UNOVIS,[28] and most likely were also responsible for ROSTA production in that city. Describing itself as a "party in art," UNOVIS attempted to link new systems of art with the revolutionary politics of the new state.[29] Abruptly juxtaposing geometric forms and explicitly political text, the Suprematist posters made for the Smolensk ROSTA and the publications section of the Revolutionary Military Council of the Western Front pose the difficult question of how to make abstraction politically effective in the most explicit terms.

UNOVIS argued (and this was a point of relative consensus among artists of the avant-garde) that the new society required new forms of representation—that artistic innovators and new systems of art had a special claim and ability to provide a voice for the new government. One UNOVIS manifesto proclaimed:

> The innovators in economic distribution, political rights, and the freedoms of man came to the Commune as the great cradle of youth and liberated it from the old lumber of prejudices and oppressions. They brought it a new meaning which awaits a new form. We, the young, are that form. WE ARE THE SUPREMACY OF THE NEW.[30]

The alliance of Suprematism and Communism represented a triumph of new over old in both art and politics, an unflinching commitment to the modern. UNOVIS understood this in generational terms: the abstract, geometric forms of Suprematism stood as a sign of the coming together of all that was young and revolutionary.

Suprematist forms were emblematic as well of an institutional alliance with the new government; for a brief moment, the avant-garde actually had power. Soon after the revolution, the cultural minister Anatolii Lunacharskii approached the Union of Artists, an organization formed in the wake of the February Revolution representing a broad artistic spectrum, seeking collaborators for the new government. After some initial hesitation, avant-garde figures like Vladimir Tatlin, Natan Al'tman, Malevich, Maiakovskii, and Rodchenko became among the first fine artists to agree to ally their efforts with the Bolsheviks.[31] The avant-garde, in turn, received control of several state agencies, including the Fine Arts section of the Commissariat of Enlightenment [IZO Narkompros], a new museum network that sent contemporary (modernist) artwork to provincial centers (including Vitebsk), and art schools and workshops (such as that in Vitebsk). The union of the forms of modernist abstraction and explicitly partisan text parallels this alliance between the avant-garde and the proletarian dictatorship— two previously marginal groups newly empowered. The flourishing of Vitebsk (and the production of experimental work in the name of the new government) was also part of a larger tendency towards decentralization during the Civil War period; in part because of a lack of far-reaching administrative control on the part of the new government, state agencies like Narkompros and the Red Army distributed funds to establish a presence in regional locations, then largely left groups to themselves.[32]

In the writing of the UNOVIS group, abstraction often stands symbolically or allegorically for a new world built on a *tabula rasa* and for a creativity unfettered by the need for adherence to an existing reality. In a 1920 essay, Lissitzky called Suprematism "a sign and symbol of this new conception of the world which comes from within us."[33] But as members of UNOVIS declared, Suprematism was also a distilled model for a new world built on the principles developed in artistic work. Structuring principles were likened to industrial and technological systems. One manifesto announced: "WE ARE THE PLAN, THE SYSTEM, THE ORGANIZATION. DIRECT YOUR CREATIVE WORK IN LINE WITH THE ECONOMY."[34]

25

Malevich called his own Suprematist works "proto-images of the technical organisms of the future Suprematist [world]."[35] Al'tman, an artist much influenced by Suprematism (as his 1923 cover for *Red Student* in this exhibition suggests [no. 52]) asserted that it was precisely the systemic quality of a work of art—the degree to which each component is bound relationally to all the others—that made it collective and proletarian. Systemization was the principle upon which "the proletariat's whole creation is constructed."[36] For Lissitzky, the integration of a work of art produced a collectivizing energy akin to electricity: "only a creative work which fills the whole world with its energy can join us together by means of its energy components like a circuit of electric current," he asserted.[37] And in Klutsis's famous early photomontage, "The electrification of the entire country," Suprematism and electrification serve as collectivizing forces in analogical combination, the aesthetic reinforcing the technological. (no. 25)

UNOVIS nurtured the belief that abstraction could serve as a binding force in the creation of a new collective spectator—a "united pictorial audience."[38] In his essay "On the 'I' and the Collective," Malevich pointed to the need for both the renunciation of the authorial subject within the work itself *and* the integration of artistic elements: "The modern saint," he wrote, "must destroy himself before the 'collective' and before that 'image' which perfects in the name of unity and the name of conjunction."[39] In practice, the Suprematist use of ruler and compass and adhesion to a set of defined geometric forms defied the definition of the artwork as an object of individual expression.

With regard to producing a collective, UNOVIS emphasized the artist's pedagogical role. Working through the art schools and workshops, the artist could teach "the masses to appreciate the things that are contemporary"[40] and produce a "universal army for a new creativity in the arts."[41] Lissitzky decreed that the artist must work "as a teacher of the new alphabet and as promoter of a world which indeed already exists in man but which he has not yet been able to perceive."[42] Freedom was defined in terms of universal creativity (and mastery of Suprematist form).

One can see the strains of the effort to make abstraction function politically in some of the Smolensk posters. One image, probably by Strzeminski, divides the visual field in two: the upper half presents the way in which four social groups should aid the front with a set of captioned, cartoon-like pictures, while an abstract Suprematist composition forms the lower half.[43] (no. 23) The two halves are graphically isolated, yet, their juxtaposition equates (in an allegorical way) the abstract composition with the collective cooperation among elements of the working class. Perhaps more effectively, another Smolensk image of unknown authorship uses the spare geometric forms of Suprematism and typographic placement and variation to reinforce the textual message. (no. 21) The small red triangle in the upper right points to the upper phrase "The organization of labor." The larger red triangle links the word "VICTORY," centrally placed and in boldface, and the lower phrase "over the capitalistic regime" in a performative way, severing the word "capitalisti-c" in an act of visual violence with symbolic resonance.

23

THE NEW ECONOMIC POLICY [NEP]

With the end of the Civil War in 1920, there was less need to advocate a Bolshevik position in competition with other groups. Victory allowed the Bolshevik Party greater control over political activity; opposition both within and without the Party was prohibited by a series of decrees, the first party purges, and mass arrests of members of rival political organizations.[44] Openly anti-Bolshevik political identification was no longer possible. In addition, the Party began to play a more direct and centralized role in cultural affairs. It replaced Narkompros and the Red Army as the most significant publisher of posters (although, on the whole, less money went into poster-making than in the immediate post-revolutionary years).[45] After the Civil War, posters show a corresponding lessening of partisan commitment. Within this narrowed spectrum, however, differing ideological positions could be staked out in subtler terms.

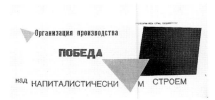

21

At the Civil War's close, the government turned to the immediate task of rebuilding the war-devastated economy. The proletariat itself—the Bolsheviks' industrial working-class political base—had been reduced to roughly half its size through factory shut-downs, mass flight to the countryside spurred by food shortages, military conscription, and promotions into the administration of the new government.[46] The peasantry, angry at forced grain requisitions, was near rebellion. The government responded pragmatically, backing away from the radical economic policies of the Civil War period and instituting a combination of measures which formed the New Economic Policy [NEP].[47] To appease the peasantry, the government ended the requisitioning of agricultural produce and replaced it with a tax-in-kind, which effectively set a limit on what could be taken. It allowed private trade in domestic markets and offered foreign investors concessions for a variety of Russian enterprises and natural resources. Recognizing the need for technical advice, the Bolshevik government also dampened the rhetoric of class struggle and encouraged "bourgeois experts"—those with useful professional training and experience such as engineers—to cooperate with the new regime. Not surprisingly, for many intellectuals who identified with the regime, NEP seemed to be an ideological capitulation.

Now that there was no longer an immediate external threat, it became necessary to combat the enemy within. In attempting to found the socialist collective within a market economy, NEP gave rise to certain inherent tensions: How would the Soviet Union be distinguished from other market economies? How could the regime mobilize bourgeois knowledge and expertise without itself becoming bourgeois? How could Soviet industrialization and technological advancement proceed without the deleterious and dehumanizing consequences for labor that had resulted with capitalist industry and technology?

The Constructivists (represented in this exhibition by artists including Rodchenko, Vavara Stepanova, and Elena Semenova, though the influence is widespread) defined themselves within the framework of NEP, developing an elaborate analogy between the artist and the engineer and thus offering their services to the state as "experts." Nonetheless, Constructivists feared the threat of embourgeoisement [*meshchanstvo*] within NEP—the possibility that nothing but the symbols had changed—and they stood vigilantly at guard against its manifestations. In the context of NEP, it was especially important (and difficult) to distinguish Soviet labor from the alienated labor of capitalism, the revolutionary commodity from the commodity fetish, and Soviet technology from the oppressive machines of the industrial revolution. The Constructivists in particular attempted to redefine these primary sites of modern conflict in their artistic work, to rid them of their pernicious aspect and develop their potential to produce an emancipated subject.

In her workers' club design, Elena Semenova attempts to do just that. (no. 57) Functioning as a room for rest, the club implies that, in contrast with workers in capitalist countries, Soviet workers belong to a leisure class. At the same time, it differentiates proletarian relaxation from contemplative bourgeois leisure. Rather than an individual occupation, such leisure is communal, the complement of collective labor. Within the club, everything is light and open, with unadorned surfaces that invoke cleanliness as much as does the sign marking the entrance to the showers on the right. Semenova's space, with its insistent reiteration of the grid and its compartmentalization of activities, is highly rationalized. Its streamlined functionalism represents, at one level, the visual expression of *use-value*—defined by Marx as an object's functional worth to human beings, an attribute often obscured in capitalism by the object's *exchange-value*, or worth on the market. And, it points to an industrial model, "based on total efficiency in every respect."[48]

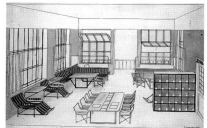

57

Like labor, the commodity was a focus of Constructivist attention. Constructivist designers were quick to volunteer their services to state agencies, now often in competition with private enterprises. The poet Maiakovskii—who solicited the collaboration with Constructivist designers like Rodchenko to produce packaging and advertising for state businesses—declared that, during NEP, progressive forces had to mobilize the instruments of capitalism against itself; and he called for the harnessing of advertising, that ultimately capitalistic form, to the interests of the collective. "Under NEP," he wrote, "it is necessary to employ all the weapons used by [our] enemies, including the advertisement, for the popularization of state, proletarian organizations, offices, and products."[49]

One poster by Rodchenko encourages investment in the new national airline with the phrase (rhyming in Russian) "He who is not a stockholder in Dobrolet [the name of the airline] is not a citizen of the USSR"—emphasizing the connection between Soviet citizenship and ownership of the means of production by urging its audience to *behave* actively as owners and invest in the material base. (no. 40) The visual presentation further reinforces the call to collective participation: an arrow begins at the punctuating dot of an attention-grabbing exclamation mark, then wraps around three sides of the poster. Moving along its length, one reads the airline's name—its trademark—then the location for stock sales, passing by an embracing message "Everyone...Everyone...Everyone...." and directly into the propeller of a schematically drawn plane. We all must assure the technological progress of the USSR, the message seems to read. What is at first surprising (but reflects the intensity of Russia's aspiration towards a technologically united population) is the urgency of this particular goal: few countries even had national airlines in the mid-twenties.

40

46a, b

Ideologically, however, Constructivist advertising vacillated between the construction of desire, necessary to sell the object, and the revolutionary imperative to circumvent fetishism. Caramel wrappers designed by Rodchenko (with verses by Maiakovskii) represent a remarkable, though perhaps ultimately unsuccessful, early effort to redefine the commodity. (no. 46a, b) The leading text "*Karamel' nasha industriia*" [which, if translated directly, would read "Caramel our industry"] can be interpreted three ways in Russian: as identifying the brand of caramel (Our Industry); as asserting the collective ownership of the means of production (The caramel is *our* industry); or as emphasizing the candy's status as the result of human labor, a foregrounding of the production relations obscured under capitalism (The caramel is [the product of] our industry.) The pictures of industrial structures on the wrappers—tram cars, steam engines, or as shown in this exhibition, bridges and grain elevators, etc.—further develop the analogy between candy manufacture and Soviet industrialization. And Maiakovskii's slogans exhort the consumer to work towards collective and collectivizing goals in rhyming couplets such as "Don't stand by the river until old age./ It's better to throw a bridge over the river." At the same time, the creation of a series of related images— tram car, steam-engine, airplane—encourages collection, a consumption mode grounded in acquisitive desire and not in the commodity's human use.

Constructivists also embraced the potential for new technological media, such as film and radio, to transform subjectivity. Dziga Vertov, a film-maker closely associated with the Constructivists, promoted the camera for this task; its "mechanical eye" could produce new, infinitely mobile perspectives bound neither by place nor time, and organize the chaos of the phenomenal world into meaningful

juxtapositions that challenged expectations and habit.[50] The Stenberg brothers'
poster for Vertov's film "The Eleventh" (commemorating the eleventh anniversary of
the Revolution) presents an image of an anamorphically elongated face of a man
wearing glasses within the frames of which appear montaged photographic frag-
ments of industrial topography, machines, and a vast crowd. In its dual suggestion
that the montaged elements are a reflection on the surface of the lenses of the external world and an image of the mind's eye, the poster invokes both the possibility of
the *reconstruction* of subjectivity through new technologies and the existence of a
new subject who sees technologically. (no. 32)

32

Rodchenko's poster for Vertov's 1924 film "Kino-Glaz" [Film- or Camera-Eye]
likewise underlines the interactive relationship between human and machine. (no.
33) In its monocular singularity, the giant central eye makes reference to the aper-
ture of the camera. At the same time, two film-cameras, both pointing downward,
define a cone of vision that emanates from the camera-eye and falls upon a pair of
photographic images, identical but reversed, of the face of a young boy. Such a
cone, drawn from a single, fixed eye, invokes the model of traditional Renaissance
perspective; the camera, it implies, is a machine for perspective, systematically
applying its laws. Yet contrary to the unidirectional gaze of traditional perspective,
here the boy(s), made subjects of the camera and straining to see, return the look.
An arrow pointing upward emphasizes the counter-directional impulse of their gaze,
while the arresting stare of the central eye implicates the spectator in this construc-
tive exchange. Repeated doubling and inversions—the structural mirroring present
in the relentless symmetry of the poster's structure—accentuate the re-productive
nature of the camera-eye.

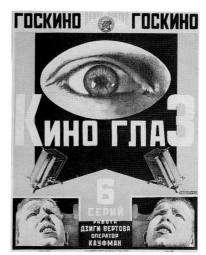

33

With Constructivist design, the confluence of technology and the production of
new subjectivity at the core of this exhibition comes into sharp relief. Indeed,
Constructivism can be best characterized by its understanding of artistic practice as
a form of technology—as the manipulation of artistic elements according to their
material character to produce an object, serving a more or less defined social function. For the Constructivists, this "function" was always, ultimately, the production of
a revolutionary subjectivity or consciousness.

Vladimir Khrakovskii, who participated in the series of debates held in 1920 and
1921 at the Institute of Artistic Culture [INKhUK] that defined the theoretical basis
of Constructivism, noted that the movement "sprang from the desire to make workers who actively create their product, to turn the mechanistically working human, the
working force, into creative workers."[51] Constructivists sought to undo the alienation
of labor still present after the revolution largely by attempting to reintegrate mental
and physical activity, art and labor, which they, following Marx, understood to have
been divided under capitalism. With theorists around them such as Viktor Shklovskii,
Osip Brik, and Boris Arvatov, they developed a model of transformative cultural practice that emphasized the role of production in changing both consciousness and the
world. They called for the radical de-hierarchicalization of the relation between artist

and viewer and for the creation of works of art that demanded labor as much in their interpretation as in their production. The artist should be a worker like any other Soviet citizen, the Constructivists insisted. And the viewer, too, should participate in the production of meaning. The work would solicit "active thinking," rather than the passive identification and contemplation of bourgeois art.[52]

Constructivist designers attempted to activize the viewer through a wide variety of visual devices including structures that produce physical movement across the surface of the work or, as in Klutsis and Sen'kin's poster "Use summer for study," (no. 49) create unstable spaces which refuse easy identification. Two planes intersect in axonometric perspective (in which orthogonal lines remain parallel, rather than converging) at the center of this work. As art historian Yve-Alain Bois has argued, axonometry creates a "radically reversible" space, setting up a figure-ground oscillation in which forms can be seen to be either protruding or receding.[53] Schematically drawn cubes adjacent to the central crossing repeat this volumetric fluctuation. Yet, Klutsis and Sen'kin set photographic elements in relation to these forms as if they possessed a certain solidity; a figure stands behind one of the intersecting planes as if it were a free-standing panel, and three workers' heads (rendered in a different scale) are positioned at reading distance. The viewer must actively negotiate through the space in this work making choices about his or her understanding of it at any one moment. In addition, he or she must select between alternate reading patterns. One can read the top word of each of the bisected planes in counter-clockwise rotation, resulting in the slogan "Use summer for study," or scan down each panel to garner more specific information about study programs.

49

Photomontage, the combining of photographs with graphic, typographic, and/or other photographic elements, was first developed as an artistic practice in the Soviet Union by Klutsis and Rodchenko. It attracted post-revolutionary artists precisely for its fragmentary, open structure, its lack of resolution into a unified visual field. Montage demanded that the viewer work relationally between elements, complementing the artist's activity with his or her own production of meaning.

However, the alternate reading choices offered by photomontage often produced tension between the Constructivist mandate for interpretative labor, and the pragmatic need for readability of a particular message. In Rodchenko's poster "I am a member of the union. The union will take care that I don't become unemployed," photographic elements aligned on each side of the caption represent two possibilities for the viewer. (no. 30) On the left, factory workers stand at their work stations, while on the right lie photographs of a line of (presumably unemployed) workers, cropped on each side to suggest its infinite length, and a fat, well-dressed couple presenting a working-class couple (identified by cap and kerchief) with alms. While the text suggests that the presentation of these alternatives is meant to encourage workers to choose an alliance with the union, their juxtaposition—their presentation as mutual possibilities—also underlines the realities of the competitive NEP market and the continuing precariousness of the worker's social position.

30

THE FIRST FIVE-PLAN PLAN

NEP effectively came to an end with the announcement in 1928 of the industrialization drive called the First Five-Year Plan. The Plan was accompanied by the forced collectivization of agriculture, intended to assure sufficient procurement of grain to offset the cost of foreign machinery needed for industrialization. Focusing on iron and steel, the Plan spurred a virtual cult of metal; investment in other sectors of the economy such as energy and transportation was often insufficient to meet the demands of metallurgical enterprises. The tractors needed for collectivized agriculture, however, were given high priority, as were giant industrial complexes like that of Magnitogorsk in the Southern Urals.[54]

A new set of elements entered the propaganda vocabulary of the posters: time, measured by the fulfillment, and increasingly the over-fulfillment, of quotas became paramount. After four-and-a-half years, the Plan was declared complete, only to be replaced with another; production goals were always out of reach. Time collapsed as workers were exhorted to fulfill the Five-Year Plan with ever-increasing speed, rendering the notion of planning obsolete. The slipperiness of the Plan is given visual form in the arithmetic of Iakov Guminer's poster "2+2 plus the enthusiasm of workers=5," where the algebraic unknown, the missing element which would close the gap left by the planner's impossible goals, is drawn from labor itself. (no. 60) The *udarnik* (m.) or *udarnitsa* (f.) was the worker, who, laboring at an constantly accelerated pace, met the Plan's demands. The root of the term—the verb *udarit'*, to strike—made the military analogy clear; the *udarniki* were the shock-troops of industry.

With the Plan's quantification of progress in terms of production goals and time tables, the chart and graph became privileged, almost iconic forms, offered as objective proof that today's exertions and privations would lead to tomorrow's hopes. Designers experimented with the visual deployment of quantitative information in order to render more immediately readable the relations between sums and their social conclusions. Charts and graphs were often embedded into the pictorial structure of the posters of the First Five-Year Plan—imaging reality through the statistical grid of economic planning. Soaring numerical figures follow the lines of the cranes in Klutsis's "We will turn the Five-Year Plan into a four-year one." (no. 61) Stacks of lumber form the component bars of a graph in Nikolai Troshin's lumber production poster, while a conveyor belt delivers planks to the top of the highest pile. (no. 64) And, in an anonymous poster, as workers pull the switch completing the electric circuit, gauges indicating a rise in productivity of labor and salaries and a decrease in the cost of manufacturing spring out from a machine balanced on an enormous number "5." (no. 69) These posters all present an image of progress in mechanized and rationalized forms, assuring the systematicity and teleological predictability of the future. Yet, these production-machines also function as a form of subterfuge by implying that the Plan's demands for increased productivity will be met by the mobilization of new technology and not by pushing workers harder.

60

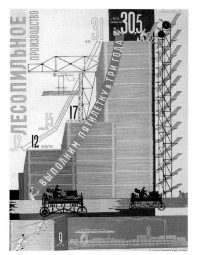

64

69

The stepped-up tempo of industrialization was matched by a reassertion of the rhetoric of class struggle, which had been tempered during NEP. The term "cultural revolution" came into wide circulation, designating a strident confrontation between the proletariat and its enemies. War metaphors, such as references to the "cultural front," "mobilization," and "work-brigades," became omnipresent. Such rhetorical images, as Sheila Fitzpatrick points out, were more than symbols; the rationing, shortages, and severe punishment of opposition and resistance that accompanied the Plan helped recreate wartime conditions.[55] Among the most common visual tropes in the graphic design of the First Five-Year Plan are groups of workers marching abreast, or lines of tractors in squadron formation.

War requires an enemy, and the bourgeois intelligentsia, only recently courted by the government during NEP, now found itself on the outside again, staring down the barrels of a newly antagonistic propaganda policy. The opening salvo came with the Shakhty trial in March 1928, when a group of mining engineers were tried and convicted of sabotage and conspiracy with foreign powers.[56] The trial implied that despite their participation in socialist construction, the intelligentsia remained a class enemy, and proletarian vigilance against a bourgeois threat was imperative. Semenova's and E. Lavinskaia's poster "We will guard the electric conductor!" invokes the danger of sabotage. (no. 74) Along with the move against bourgeois experts, the government also launched a drive against those who had profited from the NEP market and against the prosperous peasant, or *kulak*, all in the name of reclaiming the revolution for the working class. Historians have recently argued that this kind of class-war militancy and aggressive rejection of social privilege can be seen as a radical response to the popular grievances provoked by such NEP contradictions as inequality of pay, unemployment, and privileges granted to an old elite.[57] Along with it came what literary historian Katarina Clark calls the "extraordinary depreciation of intellectual expertise of all kinds."[58]

74

Complementing the renewed vigor in attacks on class enemies, the representation of the proletarian collective as a rationalized and militarized work force increasingly becomes the focus of First Five-Year Plan posters. This is particularly striking in Klutsis's "We will repay the coal debt to the country." (no. 91) Klutsis's coal miners move in synchronization as a collective, both infinite in their extension and indivisible into parts. Parity of scale and repetition of body position insistently assert the miners' collective presence, while differentiation of tools specify their interdependent functions within the collaborative endeavor. The range of ages within the group suggests a society tightly knit across generations by common purpose, and the tight shoulder-to-shoulder formation reflects the military rhetoric of the First Five-Year Plan. The use of photography, in emphasizing both the mechanical production and the reproducibility of the image, underlines this standardization of presentation. This, like many other images of the First Five-Year Plan, is an insistently machinic representation of labor with each worker functioning as a well-disciplined cog in the production system.

91

The Five-Year Plan signaled a period of proletarian hegemony, in which the working class dispensed with the mediation of the bourgeois expert and took technology for its own; in this sense, the Plan stood as sign and symbol for social mobility. As Fitzpatrick has argued, proletarian advancement into technical and administrative positions was the positive corollary to attacks on class enemies. Policies of worker promotion into management operated in conjunction with increased access to secondary, higher, and technical education to create a new "proletarian" intelligentsia.[59]

Nikolai Dolgorukov's photomontage poster "Transport worker, armed with technical knowledge, fight for the reconstruction of transport" celebrates the new proletarian expert. (no. 84) The figure's photographic head extends from its drawn torso; while a compass-wielding red arm connects the body to the technical drawing of machine components below. Behind, within a glass and steel shed rendered schematically in architectural perspective, a photographic locomotive is held aloft by a horizontal red crane. The allusive play set up between the two photographic elements, the head and the locomotive, stresses the industrial object's status as the product of the worker's rational, mental labor, while the seamless movement between photography and graphic forms lays claim to proletarian mastery over technology, a melding of the mind of the worker with the technical language of engineering. The use of red unambiguously links the arm of technical knowledge and feats of industrial prowess (such as lifting a locomotive) to the ideological structure of Communism. The transport worker thus stands as a figure of unalienated labor, simultaneously exerting mental and physical effort and able to control technology and the means of production.

On the cultural front, class-war militancy manifested itself in the rejection of social privileges, established authority, and traditional cultural values. Anatolii Lunacharskii, who had overseen Narkompros since the Revolution, was now criticized for his "anti-revolutionary, opportunist conception of cultural revolution as a peaceful, classless raising of cultural standards—a conception which does not distinguish between bourgeois and proletarian elements of culture."[60] The cultural revolution unleashed many forms of criticism of established authority. Often the youth division of an artistic organization took the lead in radicalizing the group's social commitment, criticizing and purging older members. In this period of heightened professional polemics, "proletarian" groups—who were not necessarily themselves of working class origin, but who demanded an explicit political accountability to what they saw as proletarian class interests—targeted established artists on the left and right. Widespread criticism of traditional genres spurred many painters who had previously shown little interest in mass media to begin to create posters, murals, and magazine and journal designs. And it is also in this period of virulent attack on traditional values that Stalin sold the masterpieces to Andrew Mellon that became the core of the collection at the National Gallery of Art in Washington, D.C.[61]

84

The terms of the First Five-Year Plan provoked a general reconceptualization of the traditional role of the artist. A more radical inversion of the artist-viewer relationship emerged; the artist was not only obliged to communicate to a mass audience, but also to become subordinate and answerable to it. Production goals analogous to those in the industrial sphere were set in the creative arts, and artists now tended to work on assignment from various publishing agencies rather than define their own projects. A new mobility was required of them as they traveled to construction sites, factories, and collective farms in order to participate first-hand in the work of the industrial collective. A member of the *Oktiabr'* [October] group announced proudly that "only 6 artists still work in studios, 240 are already out in factories and plants."[62] The artist's movement towards the proletariat in physical terms—to the sites of labor—was also manifested in a concept of direct accountability to the working class understood in the most literal terms: workers' letters to the editors were held up as weapons in battles between various artistic factions; Izogiz, the State Publishing House for Art, submitted poster designs to factory committees for consideration and approval; and even Narkompros, the cultural ministry, began holding meetings at production sites to hear proletarian criticism of its decisions.[63]

Designers were to participate in the work of defining a new truly mass art produced by "the artistically independent strata of the proletariat itself"—of creating a new worker-artist.[64] Many committed themselves to organizing mass artistic activities at production sites or in workers' clubs. In a work that emphasizes the imperatives of the period, short texts by worker-correspondents (non-professional journalists working within factory-based groups) accompany Rodchenko's photo-story on the AMO automobile factory in *Daesh'* [Forward], (no. 83d) a journal published in 1929 which was largely the collaborative product of members of *Oktiabr'*.

83d

Deprofessionalization of the creative arts was accompanied by a movement towards parity in wages between the worker and the artist. Under the pressure of intense criticism and facing declining forums for his work, Rodchenko reluctantly signed an agreement in 1931 to produce a certain number of photographs per month for the State Publishing House at the same rate as any worker-correspondent.[65] As the individual creator fell increasingly under suspicion as a remnant of bourgeois high culture, experiments with the collective authorship of artistic projects became commonplace; "brigades" of artists and writers descended upon industrial projects and large farms. The poster "Free working hands of the collective farms, to industry!," discussed earlier, announces itself to be the work of Brigade KGK-3. Its collective production complements its image—the crowd transformed into an equipped and well-ordered work force.

Emphasizing artists' "subordination to the task of serving the concrete needs of the proletariat," the program of the *Oktiabr'* group—a last alliance of avant-garde forces to which Boris and Elizaveta Ignatovich, Klutsis, Valentina Kulagina, Natal'ia Pinus, Rodchenko, Sen'kin, and other artists belonged—reflects the mandates of the First Five-Year Plan. *Oktiabr'* was committed to propaganda through mass media; to the organization of a collective way of life through architecture and design; and to raising the cultural level of the whole of the working class to that of "the avant-garde, the revolutionary industrial proletariat which is consciously building the socialist economy on the bases of organization, planning, and highly developed industrial technology."[66]

Yet while these aims resembled those of other groups at this time (including those of the powerful, "proletarian" groups advocating a didactic realism adapted from nineteenth-century models, such as the Association of Artists of the Revolution [AKhR] and its youth division), *Oktiabr'*s commitment to an art built on "new technological ground"[67] did not, and around this distinction spun an aesthetic and ideological maelstrom. In a continuation of the Constructivist critique of bourgeois art, *Oktiabr'* reproved AKhR for its adherence to a passive model of spectatorship in no uncertain terms: "The contemplative, static, naturalistic realism of the other groups, with their embellishment and canonization of the old way of life, sapped the energy and enervated the will of the culturally underdeveloped proletariat."[68] AKhR, in turn, attacked *Oktiabr'*s class credentials, citing its members' lack of connection to the working class, and the insufficient legibility of their work, full of "formalist" tendencies and foreign influences. Bitter polemics, as this sparring suggests, were also characteristic of the First Five-Year Plan.

THE SECOND FIVE-YEAR PLAN

The Second Five-Year Plan marked a shift away from the radicalism and contentiousness of the First, a general momentum towards normalization.[69] In 1931, a new Party slogan—"The reality of our program is active people—is you and us [together]"— signalled the waning of the technological determinism of the early years of the First Five-Year Plan and the emergence of a new conception of labor oriented around the individual worker. Delivering "six conditions for victory" in his famous speech "New Circumstances and New Tasks" at an economic conference in June of that year, Stalin rejected "vulgar egalitarianism" and called for the introduction of a wage hierarchy, the replacement of collective factory management with individual administrators, and encouraged respect for traditional experts, who, he asserted, had learned that the costs of sabotage were too high. (These conditions are enumerated on quite a few of the posters in the exhibition; designers seem to have immediately launched into action in order to activate a shift, familiarizing the population with the new marching orders.) Repudiating a collective class hegemony in favor of individual responsibility, Stalin announced the new irrelevance of the concept of class war. The Second Five-Year Plan itself, begun in 1933, set more moderate goals than did the First and stressed in its rhetoric production quality and the acquisition of skills. In visual arts, the repercussions of these changes take the form of a gradual transmutation rather than sharp demarcation.

In 1931, photomontage had been challenged in series of public forums, with critics focusing their attack on the very technicity of the medium.[70] Klutsis, for example, was censured for his mechanistic methods and his "impersonal" representation of the worker. In place of the fragmented structure of photomontage, critics demanded a new humanist realism populated with heroic individuals bound together in organic harmony.[71]

Cultural authorities attempted to stem factional battles, so exacerbated during the First Plan period, and to improve quality in the arts by subsuming various groups within broad umbrella organizations such as the Writers' and Artists' Union.[72] Poster production was consolidated under Izogiz, the State Publishing House for Art.[73] While tempering inter-group polemics, these unified associations exerted a generally conservative pressure, reasserting the authority of tradition and the professionalism of art through the definition of a practice of which only trained artists were capable. In the visual arts, the traditional genres of painting and monumental sculpture were once again valorized. A new painterly style of poster-making became prevalent, resulting in such incongruous works as Aleksei Kokorekin's "Bolsheviks must master technology," an image of a leather-garbed man riding a motorcycle rendered in soft, washed tones. (no. 101)

101

Photomontage survived the challenges of 1931, both generally and in Klutsis's work, but in changed form, its disjunctures muted and its structures hierarchicalized. In Klutsis's work, crossing from the First Five-Year Plan to the Second, there is a movement away from an imaging of the collective that stresses equality and infinite mechanical reproduction to an assertively hierarchical structure. Something of this shift in emphasis can be seen by examining two successive versions of Klutsis's design for "The reality of our program is active people—is you and us [together]," which takes its title from Stalin's "Six Conditions" speech. In the first, while the image distinguishes Stalin from the rest of the workers' corps by the prominence of his position and the difference in his dress, it insists, at the same time, on his membership within the collective. (no. 92) Distance melds the workers' corps into a unified and infinite procession, which closer inspection reveals to be composed of three repeating units, with two distinct columns of marching laborers in each. In the first column, Stalin strides alongside four smiling workers with tools slung over their shoulders, and in the second, a smaller-scale photograph of the torsos of the same four workers is overlaid with a trio of outsized legs extended out in synchrony, propelling the whole entity forward along the bright, red field. Here, the collective is figured through the repetition of anonymous bodies and the repetition of that repetition in infinite extension in a thorough-going technification of the image of labor.

92

A new conception of the heroic worker and leader emerges in a slightly later maquette for "The reality of our program...." (no. 93a) While the text enumerates Stalin's six conditions, including the condemnation of "radical egalitarianism," the image isolates one of the worker units. The separation of the single unit from the repeating series positions the two columns, large and small, front and back, in a hierarchical relation, suggesting an avant-garde and a second tier. The figure of Stalin is retouched extensively, knitting component photographic parts into an integral whole, and eliminating the seams of the montage. While in the first maquette,

93a

four torsos share three legs, in the second, a leg is aligned with each torso, insisting on the illusion of organic integrity. The first maquette's repetitive structure and disjunction within the figures underlines the constructed nature of the work, its status as representation, its reproducibility and irreality. In contrast, the excision of the single unit in the second maquette and the insistence on corporeal wholeness represents a move towards naturalization, to the reconstitution of a unified visual field. Gone is the diagonal velocity of the red field, and with it a sense of dynamic continuum extending beyond the pictorial frame. Stalin as leader comes into more prominence; his singular representation renders him irreplaceable and irreproducible.

107

Something similar happens in the distinction between Klutsis's "We will repay the coal debt to the country," (no. 91) discussed earlier, and the 1932 image "Greetings to those who have joined the work at the world-wide giant Dneprostroi DGES [Dneiper Hydro-Electric Station]. Long live the shock-workers [*udarniki*] of socialist construction." (no. 107) In contrast to the monumental workers' triad of the earlier composition, a worker-giant here rises above the hydro-electric dam, while a parade of tiny workers traverses its span. It constructs an heroic everyman who takes primacy of place in a newly hierarchic work force. The contrast between Klutsis's two posters also traces a paradigmatic shift—the replacement of aggregation with type, or of a systemic concept of collective with the exemplary individual.

We see this, as well, in Boris Belopol'skii's poster, captioned with a heavy-handed quotation from Stalin, "Strive for still greater success in the business of nurturing the female proletarian mass in the spirit of struggle for the full majesty of socialism." (no. 108) Four smiling photographic faces, retouched into anonymity, stand for general categories of labor: construction, aviation, factory work, and farming. To function in the political realm, the figure of the exemplar requires a certain generic aspect—one not so specific to be seen as a distinct (and therefore unique) individual, nor so amorphous as to offer no guidance in imagining the ideal. While the images' photographic origin lends a factual aspect to this construction of reality, the retouching banishes details which might speak for contingency or difference, and allows them to claim a status as the particular manifestation of the universal. Here, the photographic medium purports to document reality, and at the same time, is manipulated in order to conform to ideological imperatives.

108

In contrast to the extreme technification and militarization of the image of labor in the First Five-Year Plan, in the years of the Second Five-Year Plan, labor is set once again in the body. In Natal'ia Pinus's poster "Women in the collective farms are a great force," round sausage-like limbs define a emphatic solidity set in contradistinction to the poster plane. (no. 109) Whereas Constructivist photomontage of the NEP period had asked the viewer to actively negotiate between disparate elements and possible alternative meanings, the viewer is now encouraged to identify with a central figure set with a unified space (or in this case three central figures within each of three unified spaces) and to accept the image as a realistic depiction of the world.

109

At the same time, a visual calm settles. Labor is evacuated of all signs of exertion and represented in a relaxed body. In Pinus's poster, one female farmer drives her tractor in a kind of working repose, while the other, with a gentle smile on her lips, holds her scythe like a broomstick. Between the two, Stalin basks in the glow of a Party Congress. Here, the worker is integrated into a pastoral landscape, feminized and domesticated, while Stalin looks on with paternal pride. The smiles of these later works are significant as well: they imply and enforce a cheerful acceptance of social roles, a harmonious relation to the world, and a confidence in the future. In 1935, Stalin announced, "Life has become better, Life has become more joyful." In its complacency, his statement announced the end of the revolutionary era, a conviction that socialism had been achieved. A whole period of graphic design comes to a close, with the sometimes contradictory and contentious dialogues of the early Soviet years now funneled into a broad mainstream of socialist realist representation.

1   Peter Kenez, *The Birth of the Propaganda State: Soviet Methods of Mass Mobilization, 1917–29* (London: Cambridge University Press, 1985), 122.

2   Kendall Bailes, *Technology and Society Under Lenin and Stalin: Origins of the Soviet Technical Intelligentsia, 1917–1941* (Princeton: Princeton University Press, 1978), 49.

3   Walter Benjamin, "One-Way Street," in *One-Way Street and Other Writings*, Edmund Jephcott and Kingsley Shorter, trans. (London: Verso, 1979), 104; cit. Susan Buck-Morss, "City as Dreamworld and Catastrophe," *October* 73 (Summer 1995): 14.

4   El Lissitzky, "Suprematism in World Reconstruction," in John Bowlt, ed., *Russian Art of the Avant-Garde: Theory and Criticism, 1902–34*, 2nd ed. (London: Thames and Hudson, 1988), 154.

5   Leon Trotskii, "Culture and Socialism," in Leon Trotskii, *Problems of Everyday Life and Other Writings on Culture and Science* (New York: Monad Press, 1973), 229.

6   Quoted in Hubertus Gassner, "The Constructivists: Modernism on the Way to Modernization," in The Guggenheim Museum, *The Great Utopia: The Russian and Soviet Avant-Garde* (New York: The Solomon R. Guggenheim Museum, 1992), 316.

7   Leon Trotskii, "Science in the Task of Socialist Construction," in Trotskii, *Problems of Everyday Life*, op. cit., 201.

8   Kenez, *The Birth of the Propaganda State*, op. cit., 70.

9   *Vos'moi s"ezd RKP(b) mart 1919 goda. Protokoly* (Moscow: 1959), 390, 394; cit. Stephen White, *The Bolshevik Poster* (New Haven: Yale University Press, 1988), 18.

10   *Pravda* (6 October 1918); cit. White, *The Bolshevik Poster*, op. cit., 112.

11   El Lissitzky, "Unser Buch," quoted in Benjamin Buchloh, "Faktura to Factography," in Annette Michelson et al, eds., *October: The First Decade* (Cambridge: MIT Press, 1987), 94. A slightly abridged version of the full text, translated into English, is included in Sophie Lissitzky-Küppers, ed., *El Lissitzky: Life, Letters, Texts* (Greenwich, CT: New York Graphic Society, 1968), 356–359.

12   White, *The Bolshevik Poster*, op. cit., vi.

13   Kenez, *The Birth of the Propaganda State*, op. cit., 96.

14   Ibid., 101.

15   White, *The Bolshevik Poster*, op. cit., 43.

16   Sheila Fitzpatrick, *The Russian Revolution*, 2nd ed. (Oxford: Oxford University Press, 1994), 70.

17   Ibid., 155.

18   For Moor's biography see White, *The Bolshevik Poster*, op. cit., 42.

19   For a discussion of the Bolshevik use of radio to produce a collective subject see Maria Gough, "Switched On," in this volume.

20   B.D. Duvakin, "Okna ROSTA i Glavpolitprosveta," in Vladimir Maiakovskii, *V.V. Maiakovskii. Polnoe sobranie socheninii*, vol. 3 (Moscow: Khudozhestvennaia literatura, 1957), 471.

21   Ibid., 473.

22   Maiakovskii, "Revoliutsionnyi plakat," in *V.V. Maiakovskii*, op. cit., vol. 12, 34.

23   White, *The Bolshevik Poster*, op. cit., 77, 80; Maiakovskii, "Revoliutsionnyi plakat," 33–35 and "Proshu slova," in *V.V. Maiakovskii*, op. cit, vol. 12, 207–208.

24 Maiakovskii, "Tol'ko ne vospominaniia," in *V.V. Maiakovskii*, op. cit., vol. 12, 153.

25 White, *The Bolshevik Poster*, op. cit., 81.

26 S.I. Stykalin, *Okna satiry ROSTA* (Moscow: Izdatel'stvo Moskovskogo Universiteta, 1976), 28; White, *The Bolshevik Poster*, op. cit., 84.

27 Fitzpatrick, *The Russian Revolution*, op. cit., 94. On Kronstadt also see Paul A. Avrich, *Kronstadt, 1921* (Princeton: Princeton University Press, 1970) and Israel Getzler, *Kronstadt, 1917–21: The Fate of a Social Democracy* (New York: Cambridge University Press, 1983).

28 Larissa Zhadova, *Malevich: Suprematism and Revolution in Russian Art*, Alexander Lieven, trans. (London: Thames and Hudson, 1982), fn. 26, 129.

29 *Al'manakh UNOVIS, no. 2*; reproduced in Zhadova, *Malevich: Suprematism and Revolution*, op. cit., 312.

30 "From UNOVIS—the champions of the new art," in Zhadova, *Malevich: Suprematism and Revolution*, op. cit., 297.

31 For this narrative see Gassner, "The Constructivists: Modernism on the Way to Modernization," in The Guggenheim Museum, *The Great Utopia*, op. cit., 301–302.

32 Katarina Clark, "The 'Quiet' Revolution in Soviet Intellectual Life," in Sheila Fitzpatrick et al, *Russia in the Era of NEP: Explorations in Society and Culture* (Bloomington: Indiana University Press, 1991), 218.

33 Lissitzky, "Suprematism in World Reconstruction," in Bowlt, ed., *Russian Art of the Avant-Garde*, op. cit., 153.

34 "From UNOVIS—the champions of the new art," in Zhadova, *Malevich: Suprematism and Revolution*, op. cit., 297.

35 Kazimir Malevich, *Suprematizm. 34 risunka* (Vitebsk: Unovis, 1920), 2; cit. Aleksandra Shatshikh, "Unovis: Epicenter of the New World," in The Guggenheim Museum, *The Great Utopia*, op. cit., 59.

36 Natan Al'tman, "Futurism and Proletarian Art," in Bowlt, ed., *Russian Art of the Avant-Garde*, op. cit., 163.

37 Lissitzky, "Suprematism in World Reconstruction," in Bowlt, ed., *Russian Art of the Avant-Garde*, op. cit., 158.

38 "From UNOVIS—the champions of the new art," in Zhadova, *Malevich: Suprematism and Revolution*, op. cit., 297.

39 Malevich, "O 'ia' i kollektive," *Al'manakh Unovis No. 1*, 1, 60b; cit. Shatskikh, "Unovis," in The Guggenheim Museum, *The Great Utopia*, op. cit., 56.

40 "For the Program" in Zhadova, *Malevich: Suprematism and Revolution*, op. cit., 311.

41 "From UNOVIS—the champions of the new art" in Zhadova, *Malevich: Suprematism and Revolution*, op. cit., 298.

42 Lissitzky, "Suprematism in World Reconstruction," in Bowlt, ed., *Russian Art of the Avant-Garde*, op. cit., 158.

43 In conversation with me, Peter Nisbet has raised the possibility that this poster was intended to have been cut in two, forming two separate posters; he points in particular to the repetition of the Smol[ensk] ROSTA insignia. However, the abstract forms swirling around an empty space would not at first glance appear to function as an autonomous political poster. A possible explanation is provided by an examination of some other Suprematist posters not featured in this exhibition. For example, the same Suprematist composition in the abstract portion of this poster forms the basis of a poster also attributed to Strzeminski, which bears the caption "An increase in production, an increase in progress is the best guarantee of success on the front." (Illustrated in Zhadova, *Malevich*, op. cit., n. 172.) The same composition appears yet again in a poster with the caption, "What have you done for the front? Give your last to those who are dying defending you." (Illustrated in Dawn Ades, *The 20th-Century Poster: Design of the Avant-Garde* [New York: Abbeville Press, 1984], 48.) The repetition of this image with varying texts suggests the possibility that it functioned to provide a unifying frame (and a Suprematist context) for a set of contingent messages.

44 Fitzpatrick, *The Russian Revolution*, op. cit., 96–102.

45 Katarina Clark describes such a phenomenon in cultural life in general. Clark, "The 'Quiet' Revolution," in Fitzpatrick et al, *Russia in the Era of NEP*, op. cit., 212–213.

46 Fitzpatrick, *The Russian Revolution*, op. cit., 94.

47 See description in Fitzpatrick, *The Russian Revolution*, op. cit., 93-96; also see Lewis Siegelbaum, *Soviet State and Society between Revolutions, 1918–1929* (Cambridge: Harvard University Press, 1992) and Fitzpatrick et al, *Russia in the Era of NEP*, op. cit.

48 A. Lavinskii, "Engineerism," doc. 23 in Henry Art Gallery, *Art into Life: Russian Constructivism, 1914–32* (New York: Rizzoli, 1990), 81.

49   Maiakovskii, "Agitatsiia i reklama," in *V.V. Maiakovskii*, op. cit., vol. 12, 57.

50   Vertov was a member, along with Constructivists such as Rodchenko and Stepanova, of the Lef group, a loose alliance of artists and theorists which formed around the journals *Lef* [Left] (1923–25) and *Novyi lef* [New Left] (1927–28). For Vertov's film theory, see Annette Michelson, ed., *Kino-Eye: The Writings of Dziga Vertov*, Kevin O'Brien, trans. (Berkeley: University of California Press, 1984).

51   Vladimir Khrakovskii in "Transcript of the Discussion of Comrade Stepanova's Paper 'On Constructivism,'" doc. 22 in Henry Art Gallery, *Art into Life*, op. cit., 75.

52   Varvara Stepanova, "On Constructivism," doc. 21 in Henry Art Gallery, *Art into Life*, op. cit., 74.

53   Yve-Alain Bois, "El Lissitzky: Radical Reversibility," *Art in America* vol. 76, no. 4 (April 1988): 161–180; especially 172–175.

54   Fitzpatrick, *The Russian Revolution*, op. cit., 130–131.

55   Ibid., 120.

56   On the Shakty trial, see Kendall Bailes, *Technology and Society under Lenin and Stalin* (Princeton: Princeton University Press, 1978).

57   See, for example, Fitzpatrick, "Cultural Revolution as Class War," 17, 34 and other essays in Sheila Fitzpatrick, ed., *Cultural Revolution in Russia, 1928–1931* (Bloomington: Indiana University Press, 1978).

58   Katarina Clark, "Engineers of Human Souls in an Age of Industrialization: Changing Models, 1929–1941," in Lewis Siegelbaum and William Rosenberg, eds. *Social Dimensions of Soviet Industrialization* (Bloomington: Indiana University Press, 1993), 252.

59   See Fitzpatrick, "Stalin and the Making of a New Elite," in Fitzpatrick, ed., *The Cultural Front. Power and Culture in Revolutionary Russia* (Ithaca: Cornell University Press, 1992).

60   Fitzpatrick, "Cultural Revolution as Class War," in Fitzpatrick, ed., *Cultural Revolution in Russia*, op. cit., 10.

61   For a narrative of the sale of masterpieces from the Hermitage to Andrew Mellon, see Robert Williams, *Russian Art and American Money* (Cambridge: Harvard University Press, 1980), 147–190.

62   Hubertus Gassner, "Heartfield's Moscow Apprenticeship," in Peter Pachnicke and Klaus Honnef, eds., *John Heartfield* (New York: Harry Abrams, 1992), 259.

63   Fitzpatrick, "Cultural Revolution as Class War," in Fitzpatrick, ed., *Cultural Revolution in Russia*, op. cit., 32; also Gassner, "Heartfield's Moscow Apprenticeship," in Pachnike and Honnef, eds., *John Heartfield*, op. cit., 258.

64   Gassner, "Heartfield's Moscow Apprenticeship," in Pachnicke and Honnef, eds., *John Heartfield*, op. cit., 259.

65   Aleksandr Lavrent'ev, *Rodchenko: Rakursy* (Moscow: Iskusstvo, 1992), 169.

66   "October—Association of Artistic Labor Declaration," in Bowlt, ed., *Russian Art of the Avant-Garde*, op. cit, 276.

67   Ibid.

68   Ibid., 277.

69   The idea that the Second Five-Year Plan marks a movement away from the militarization of the First Plan towards normalization is the thesis of scholars such as Katerina Clark and Sheila Fitzpatrick. See Fitzpatrick, *The Russian Revolution*, op. cit.,148–172 and Clark, "Engineers of Human Souls," in Siegelbaum and Rosenberg, eds., *Social Dimensions of Soviet Industrialization*, op. cit., 248–264. In the visual arts, Hubertus Gassner begins to define a shift from the emphasis on technics in the early years of the First Five-Year Plan to a new humanistic conception of labor after 1931. Gassner, "Heartfield's Moscow Apprenticeship," in in Pachnicke and Honnef, eds., *John Heartfield*, op. cit., 270–271.

70   These important debates are discussed in Gassner, "Heartfield's Moscow Apprenticeship," in Pachnicke and Honnef, eds., *John Heartfield*, op. cit., 256–289.

71   Ibid., 265–266.

72   Katarina Clark argues that the Party's action in dissolving independent artistic groups in 1932 should be understood in terms of a renewed interest in literary quality in the aftermath of the extremism of the First Five-Year Plan. See "Little Heroes and Big Deeds: Literature Responds the First Five-Year Plan," in Fitzpatrick, ed., *Cultural Revolution in Russia*, op. cit., 189–206, especially 204.

73   In Ivan Matsa, ed., *Sovetskoe iskusstvo za 15 let: materialy i dokumentasiia* (Moscow-Leningrad: Ogiz-Izogiz, 1933), 643–644.

Switched On: Notes on Radio, Automata, and the Bright Red Star*

MARIA GOUGH

I

Building the Collective opens with a pair of visual metaphors that convey the historical opposition in early twentieth-century Russia of two modes of societal organization: the pyramid of autocratic stratification (Aleksei Radakov's "Autocratic structure," published in Petrograd between the revolutions of 1917 [no. 2]), and the red star of the communist collective (Dmitrii Moor's "Soviet Russia is a camp under siege. Everyone to the defense!" produced at the height of the Civil War in September 1919 [no. 1]). In an exhortation to the defense of the besieged Soviets, Moor's poster adumbrates a visual metaphor of collective organization that was, historically, distinctly opposed to that order which Radakov satires.

By drawing upon an established convention for the description of social hierarchy—the pyramid of strata—Radakov swiftly secures a community of legibility for his satirical description of the structure of Tsarist autocracy. In terms of the history of illegal anti-Tsarist propaganda in particular, this convention is said to have been founded by N. N. Lokhov's drawing "The Social Pyramid," published in Geneva in 1901 and widely disseminated through postcard reproductions and variations.[1] In Radakov's poster, a ticker-tape chant of autocracy provides a running explanation, in descending order, of the function of each stratum enveloped under

39

the protective royal ermine: "We rule you" (the Tsar enthroned), "We pray for you" (the ecclesiastical elite), "We judge you" (the judiciary), "We defend you" (the military), "We feed you" (the land-owning gentry and industrialists), and finally, the acrid conclusion to this altruistic beneficence: "And you work." The "you" of the address are revealed along the pyramid's base: the proletarian, the peasants, and the infantry soldier, down-trodden and crushed by the weight of the fat men ("the enemy was almost invariably fat," Nina Tumarkin writes[2]) stacked upon them. Radakov tips the conventional pyramid perspectively so that the ascension upwards is also a movement into depth, thus producing an inversion of scale which highlights both the severity of the oppression of the lowest stratum of the hierarchy, and the distant, inaccessible remove of state power.

2

In Moor's "Soviet Russia is a camp under siege. Everyone to the defense!," which was commissioned by the Revolutionary Military Council in an edition of 20,000,[3] the collective defense of Soviet Russia against the White armies is orchestrated by the red star of the Bolsheviks. Unlike the pyramid, the star, according to Richard Stites, "has no prehistory in the Russian radical tradition" (although it may have been inspired by Aleksandr Bogdanov's 1908 Martian-Marxian epic *Red Star*). The dissemination of the star, from its debut in 1918 in the form of a Red Army breast badge (comprising a crossed hammer and plough) to its prompt migration to the flag of Soviet Russia by the end of the same year, represents a self-conscious attempt to establish a new symbology dedicated to the advocacy of the fledgling Bolshevik state.[4]

1

Moor demonstrates considerable graphic force and purpose in combining this newly inaugurated symbol—the flat, red, five-pointed star (the idiosyncratic symmetry of which figures the revolution's protest against stasis)—with older representational systems derived from Russian pictorial tradition, namely, those of the icon and *lubok* [folk engraving]. The headquarters of the Workers' and Peasants' Defense is depicted in a central tondo: a worker, a peasant, and a Red Army man deliberate strategy, maps spread before and behind them. The city of Moscow, the seat of the Bolshevik government since the Russian capital moved from Petrograd in March of 1918, is marked in the center of the map spread upon the table, serving also to pinpoint the center of the star itself. The "trinity" of strategists is somewhat cramped by the tondo's circumference into a space ordered according to a pictorial system which flourished in Byzantium: the scrolled maps heaped under the table "project" almost vertically to the surface plane, thus evoking the tilted depth of Byzantine representation. The poster counts upon, as it were, the stimulation in the spectator of a kind of Rublevian memory trace.

The star's radiating arms divide up the collectively decided upon tasks of the Workers' and Peasants' Defense into separate vignettes, while its two upper points also serve to rebuff the dark shadows plaguing the Soviets: the winged skeleton of death driving the chariot of *golod* [hunger] on the left, and the fat bird-man capitalist holding the chain-reins of the chariot of *rabstvo* [slavery, servitude] on the right. Only the sum of these vignettes, the collective effort, will ensure the success of the

Defense. Clockwise from the lower left, the scroll recounts this effort: "the woman takes the place of the fighter who has gone to the front" (a peasant woman takes on the duties of the village points-man); "the worker forges weapons"; "the Communist points out the enemy and leads into battle"; "the peasant delivers the bread"; and "youth learn soldiering." While the flat stamp of the red star divides up the field and its depicted activity into parts of equal value, an illusionistic system loosely derived from the *lubok* is also at work: the scrolling annotation charts the circumference of the sun rising protectively over the territory of the commune, repelling the forces of darkness in the rear, while the crenellated walls of the fortressed commune enclose and defend it against the enemy's frontal siege.

By this well-orchestrated conjunction of new and older representational systems, Moor's poster proposes an emphatic association of the Bolshevik project of building the collective (which is not named but implicit) with the enclosed communal arcadia of the pre-revolutionary peasant *mir* [village community]. In trying to find a means by which to articulate the solidarity of the new collective, Moor presents, in the weaving together of old and new and with the absence of any conspicuous trace of imported Western representational systems, a eulogy to the "socially exposed particularity" of labor in the primitive commune.[5] But it is the red star of the Bolsheviks which maps the poster's pictorial field; the military insignia totalizes the commune, orchestrating its Defense. The rapid shot of the poster medium (what Nikolai Tarabukin describes as its likeness to "a lightening charge, a sudden attack, a manoeuvre of cavalry in battle"[6]) is here thickened, slowed, stabilized: the poster unfurls the flag of revolution, the badge worn over the heart of every Red Army man.

A somewhat later work, "The Red Army is the fighting school of the workers" (author unknown, n.d., no. 68), exploits the star-as-mapping-device: by means of its own infinite repetition, the military insignia rigidly demarcates the Red Army's myriad activities. It is difficult to resist teleologising these early works in terms of the suppressed violence of powerful images such as Vavara Stepanova's photomontage for the 1938 album "*Krasnaia armia*,"[7] in which the portrait of a military dignitary fills the star's central tondo. A whole phalanx of infantry advance in radial formation, set into motion by the figure of the star which consumes its collective singular subject in an anonymous acting-out of the will of its center.[8] The trajectory taken by the star in Soviet graphic production of the inter-war period bears out the profound ambiguity already contained within Moor's early example, namely, that the star represents both the collective, and at the same time, that to which the collective was opposed, the stratified imperium: each of the star's radiating points is also a rotated pyramid. In other words, its graphic ambiguity figures the oscillation, or contradiction, between communality and hierarchy that underscores the project of building a socialist future.

"Soviet Russia is a camp under siege. Everyone to the defense!" provides illustrative testimony to the Bolshevik faith in the tenacity of its systemic model for the organization of the new *Soviet* Russia. The collective of communism, in which plurality is always singular, is advanced as the most perfect mode of organization,

68

the ideology of which is so fundamental and pervasive in Russian that it "may not require separate translation."[9] The concern to eliminate superfluous and arbitrary elements—to excise the fat men—is an abiding obsession of the early Bolshevik period which is manifest in all fields of its endeavor.[10] With this faith comes also a very problematic, and probably unresolvable, relation to the articulation of difference, to the manifestation of diversion or digression. The Bolsheviks' *politika* of centralized leadership, planning, and administration, also poses problems for its ideology of the collective that are, similarly, not so easily resolved, hence the significance of Moor's invocation of the peasant commune as the scenography of his poster's exhortation to the collective, centrally-directed, Defense. It may be that, as a result of the contradiction posed by centralization, the "collective" is one of the most truly mythic aspects of the Bolshevik enterprise.

II

If the immediate task was to transform the plural into the singular, how was this collective phenomenon, both real and "imagined" in Benedict Anderson's sense, to be brought about? What were the tools and materials of its construction? To a significant extent the answer was thought to lie within the realm of technology (of which the lithography of the poster medium is in itself a profound example), but particularly in the longed-for deployment of the innovations of the second industrial revolution, especially that of electricity, across *all* of Soviet Russia. Lenin's policy of "Communism equals Soviet power plus electrification of the entire country" is perhaps the proverbial equation of the 1920s.[11] This phrase occasioned one of Gustav Klutsis's first attempts to merge an iconography of Bolshevik policy with the fine axonometric and planimetric intarsia of his early series of "dynamic cities," namely, a photocollage (no. 25)[12] prepared in 1920 as a design for a poster entitled "The electrification of the entire country." This is an explicit example of the confluence of Bolshevik and avant-garde enthusiasm for electrification and network technologies as the heralds of a bright Red future.

25

Of the diversity of ways in which the role of technology in the building of the collective was speculatively framed in the early Bolshevik period, I would like to consider just two. The first concerns the deployment of a specific technological advance, namely, that of the radio, focusing on a 1921 text by the futurist poet Velemir Khlebnikov, entitled, "Rosta budushchego" [the ROSTA of the future]. The second way has less to do with technological innovation *per se*, and more with an absorption of the technological as the figure of all socialist endeavor: the building of the collective through the mechanization and automatization of labor, irrespective of whether that labor be physical, mechanical, or mental. I focus on the elaboration of the notion of *ustanovka* [positioning] as a key device for the instantiation of the mechanized collective, by that other "poet" of the revolution, whom Nikolai Aseev lyricised as the "Ovid of engineers, miners, and metal-workers,"[13] namely, Aleksei Gastev.

First, the poet and the radio: Khlebnikov spent the winter months of 1920–21, from October to March, in the Caucasian town of Piatigorsk as the night-watchman of its Press building, in which were also housed the offices of the Russian Telegraph Agency [ROSTA] of Terskaia province. There he wrote verse, 1,200 copies of which the journal *Stennaia Rosta* pasted up throughout the region. According to one of the poet's later publicists, Khlebnikov would often visit the Agency's radio receiving station in order to study its operations.[14] During this winter Khlebnikov wrote a visionary account of the "infinite tasks" of the future Russian Telegraph Agency, which he entitled "Rosta budushchego" [the ROSTA of the future]. The manuscript remained unpublished until 1927, when it appeared in the popular monthly *Krasnaia nov'*, short of its original opening paragraphs and with a significantly altered title, namely, "Radio budushchego" [the *Radio* of the future]. It is this 1927 title which has stuck.[15]

By "radio," Khlebnikov is referring less to broadcast as we understand it today, and more to the transmission of coded signals such as Morse by wireless telegraph [*besprovolochnyi telegraf*, or "Тбр"]. 1921 is in fact the very moment of the latter technology's transformation into, or reinvention as, broadcast. The expressions "wireless telegraph" and "radiotelegraph" are synonyms, but at some point in the teens, "telegraph" was dropped from the latter for economy's sake, and the suffix "radio" thus came to stand alone. However in 1921, "radio" did not *yet* mean broadcast; radio broadcasting got underway at the state level in Russia only at the end of 1922, while regular programming did not commence until 1924. It is important to note the historical development of radio technology so as not to diminish the prophetic nature of Khlebnikov's vision of the future of ROSTA. For Khlebnikov is less interested in how things stand in 1921, and more in how they will be in the future. In this sense then, the later editorial substitution of radio for ROSTA destroys much of the speculative quality and historical piquancy of the poet's thinking.

In the original version, Khlebnikov concedes that for the time being ROSTA already has its job cut out for it, contributing to the "rigorous struggle" of the present day (a reference to the military deployment of the wireless telegraph that had led both to the expansion of the technology itself and also to the creation of a new *art* of warfare). The so-called "ROSTA poster," several examples of which appear in the present exhibition, is a *material* trace of the Agency's role, in collaboration with artists and poets of left persuasion, in the Bolshevik struggle.[16] While the official decrees publicized by ROSTA posters were more likely to have been culled from published newspaper reports, the telegraph was the most immediate source for the latest news from the front, and from the capital for those stationed in the provinces as was Khlebnikov. Although wired telegraph transmission was still in usage in ROSTA's offices, and even had certain advantages over the newer technology (such as privacy of transmission), it was only the wire*less* telegraph which encompassed the possibility of broadcast (although, as yet, static interference still hindered the latter's successful transmission of the human voice).

Khlebnikov prophesies however a different future for the Agency: "One can compare ROSTA of the future with the consciousness of the human being, with his brain. This is the universal, strong-willed rallying-point of the people, which sends out to [the people], along innumerable paths and channels, [the people's] own will, administering to it jolts and blows." These two final words refer to the dots and dashes of telegraphic transmission as lightening bolts (i.e. electricity) and thunder claps.[17] Khlebnikov's vision enumerates the new spatial and cultural forms which will be generated by the radiotelegraph of the future, namely: "Radioreadingrooms," "Radioauditoria," "Radioexhibitions," "Radioclubs," and several miscellaneous achievements of the radio as "Great Magician." Their combined operation will forge human consciousness into a singular collective subject. In the poet's account, a picture begins to emerge of the double agitation of the radio of the future: of its contemporaneous work of diffusion and dissemination on the one hand, and of collectivization and centralization on the other.

The Radioreadingroom is an improvement, in magnitude and coverage, on the already existing propaganda media of wall newspapers [stengazety] and wall ROSTAs [stennaia Rosta]. "With the help of lightening" (Khlebnikov's naturalizing metaphor for "electricity," a word which appears nowhere in this text), the radio has solved the "problem of celebrating the communion of humanity's universal soul, one daily spiritual wave...washes over the entire country every twenty-four hours, saturating it with a flood of scientific and artistic news."[18] Each town and settlement will have its own Radioreadingroom, each identical to the other, which will take the form of a gigantic "book of the street" mounted in every village square. Upon the pages [polotnakh (literally, "canvasses")] of this book will be printed the latest waves of information received by the local station, which will be, again, identical everywhere.

In the outdoor Radioauditorium, where "the iron mouth of the automatic voice [samoglasa]...has transformed the surge of lightening into amplified spoken language, into singing and human speech," the village reading collective will become also a listening one.[19] The Radioreadingrooms will also function as Radioexhibitions, the pages of the giant books becoming projection screens for the color transmission of images by means of light impulses beamed from Moscow. The Radio's universal ear is thus transformed into "eyes, for whom there is no distance." (Kazimir Malevich's dream of the arterialization of the entire country with exhibitions of contemporary art, radiating out from Moscow to the provinces, finds here its earliest televisual equivalent.[20]) Radioclubs will organize the activities of leisure across the entire world: international chess-games, trans-Atlantic conversations, singing in unison.[21] The Radio as "Great Magician" will transmit sensations of taste (water will taste as wine), odors, medical treatments without medicine (such as hypnosis), and it will organize education, sending out lessons and lectures to every school.[22] Thus will be brought about, Khlebnikov concludes, "the unification of [the country's] consciousness into a single will....Radio [will] forge the continual links in the universal soul, and mold mankind into a single entity"[23] Through radio broadcast, the consciousness of the provinces will be forged into collective solidarity with the capital, thus helping to mitigate what was, for the Bolshevik leadership, the politically very costly gulf between the city and the country-side. The "center," however, will always remain the master of the universal soul: while in the Readingreading room there had still been the possibility of "each read[ing] what he wants to read,"[24] this possibility decreases in inverse proportion to the increasing feasibility of broadcast.

Khlebikov refers to "the entire country," and occasionally to "the entire world," but not once does he refer to Russia by name, thereby keeping alive the possibility of the whole world as a single unity. In a letter of 1920, Lenin describes the radio as a "newspaper without paper and 'without borders.'"[25] Indeed broadcast was to become a major tool in the implementation of the Bolsheviks' early policy of "international socialism" (which held that crucial to the success of the Bolshevik revolution in Russia was the assistance of the more industrially advanced European nations, which in turn depended upon the spread of revolution abroad). The early 1920s witnessed the intense activity of the Komintern (also known as the "Third" or "Communist International") to the glory and memory of which Vladimir Tatlin's tower, although ini-tially commissioned as a "monument to the *revolution*," was dedicated by the time of its completion in November 1920. Hence, its title became "The Monument to the Third International." Tatlin crowned this model of the Komintern's headquarters with a rotating radio station for the future broadcast of Radio Komintern. In 1922 Klutsis designed "radio-orators" [*radio-oratory*] to be stationed along Tverskoi Boulevard for the immediate dissemination of reports from the Fourth Congress of the Komintern, which was meeting in Moscow in September of that year. Radio Komintern made its first international broadcasts at the end of 1922 from the Shabalovka Radio Tower in Moscow, which was designed by the engineer-architect Vladimir Shukhov to tower with visionary force over a district populated by single-story wooden structures.[26] It is the Shabalovka Tower which is cut out of its neighborhood to stand at Lenin's right hand in a poster of 1925 by Yulian Shutskii, entitled "Radio. From the will of millions we will create a single will." (no. 31) The confluence of Khlebnikov's early specula-tive vision and Bolshevik policy of the mid 1920s is explicit. Utilizing the formal vocab-ularies of constructivism and suprematism, a scaffolding of photomontage and col-lage elements presents the network components of radio transmission, and its effects. The disruptions of scale produced by the montage are re-absorbed by the network constitutive of radio technology. In the abstract space of the red square, however, one will is afforded significantly more force in the constitution of the single collective will.[27]

Thus, by the time of its publication in 1927, the future has caught up with Khlebnikov's vision. ROSTA has become Radio, and broadcast is in full swing as a splendid ideological tool. The radio became an instrument in the consolidation of the *Union* of Soviet Socialist Republics out of its various republics and autonomous territories, a process which began at the end of the Civil War. Moor's "Peoples of the Caucasus!" (1920, no. 6) dates to the inception of this process, which Lewis

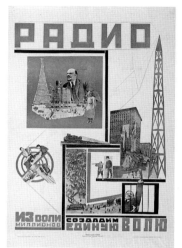

31

Siegelbaum terms the "in-gathering of the nations" according to a "common con-sciousness of class as opposed to...national, religious, or ethnic identities,"[28] culmi-nating in the Stalinist doctrine of "socialism in one country," which replaced the early Bolshevik policy of international socialism in the mid 1920s.

In a 1926 address to the First All-Union Congress of the Society of Friends of the Radio, which was published just a few months before Khlebnikov's vision in the pages of the same journal *Krasnaia nov'*, Trotskii argues that it is precisely "because Turkmenistan is *far* [that] it ought to be *near*....We cannot seriously talk about social-ism without having in mind the transformation of the country into a single whole, linked together by means of all kinds of communications....Our radio communica-tions have brought nearer the transformation of Europe into a single economic orga-nization. The development of a radiotelegraphic network is...a preparation for the moment when the people of Europe [i.e. Soviet Europe] and Asia shall be united in a Soviet Union of Socialist Peoples."[29] In the shift in Bolshevik policy from the inter-national dissemination of socialism to its national fortification, one witnesses a shift in the official conception of the *potentiality* of radio: from being an instrument of infinite and thus borderless expansion, to that of the centralizing consolidation of "the country as a single whole."

The final aspect of Khlebnikov's vision of the "radio collective" that I would like to note is his enthusiasm for economy in language, time, and labor productivity. The original manuscript opens with a defense of linguistic economy: "The word ROSTA arose through the merging into a single word of the initial sounds of the following three words: *Rossiiskoe Telegrafnoe Agenstvo* [Russian Telegraph Agency]. Mankind still has the same 365 days as had the caveman. It is cramped in its 365 days; not knowing how to lengthen the year, it rejects long-sounding words. In this regard the Russian language has made a courageous leap forward [*smelyi skachok*], adopting short artificial words, such as ROSTA."[30] The concise and elliptical style in which telegrams are worded, known as "telegraphese," signifies the predilection for an extreme or radical economy, the absence, that is, of superfluous elements. Word abbreviation is posed by the futurist poet as the solution to temporal shortage.

With regard to labor productivity: Khlebnikov builds upon the "known fact" that "certain sounds, like 'lia' and 'si,' increase muscular capacity, sometimes as much as sixty-four times, strengthening it for a certain period." Khlebnikov envisages radio broadcast as a kind of sonic Cybex®, a rousing singing to the nation's collective musculature: "On days of intensified labor, summer harvests, the con-struction of great buildings, these sounds will be sent out by the Radio across the entire country, manifoldly increasing its strength."[31] Khlebnikov's fantastic proposal for the raising of the productivity of labor presages those scenes which Aleksandr Rodchenko among others was to photograph a decade later: a prison orchestra, playing to the labor gangs enslaved in the construction of Stalin's terrible project, the White Sea Canal. Ultimately, Khlebnikov's double fantasy of the Radio as the magi-cian of "extension," of both muscles and the year, finds its most extreme and brutal expression in the great pre-stakhanovite achievement of the accelerated fulfillment of the Five-Year Plans: Klutsis's "We will turn the Five-Year Plan into a four-year one" (no. 99) and Iakov Guminer's ode to the "Arithmetic of the Counter-Plan: 2 + 2 plus the enthusiasm of workers=5."[32] (no. 60)

18

III

The call for the "scientific organization of labor" [*nauchnaia organizatsiia truda*, or NOT] was an important aspect of the Bolsheviks' response to the various "discrepancies" [*nozhnitsy* (literally, "scissors")[33]] which plagued Soviet Russia's infant economy, such as that between the productivity of labor and its wage remuneration, or, the recurrent imbalance between levels of industrial and agricultural production that is addressed by Vladimir Kozlinskii's ROSTA, "Work and there will be flour. Sit with crossed arms and there will not be flour [*muká*] but suffering [*múka*]," of 1921. (no. 18) With important differences, NOT is the Soviet version of Western scientific management and draws explicitly upon the work of Taylor, Ford, the Gilbreths and others. In "The Immediate Tasks of the Soviet Government," (1918) Lenin calls for the "raising of the productivity of labor" and the securing of its better organization. Revoking his earlier hostility to Western scientific management, Lenin proposes debate on the "application...of what is scientific and progressive in the Taylor system," which he describes as "the combination of the refined brutality of bourgeois exploitation and a number of the greatest scientific achievements in the field of analyzing mechanical motions during work, the elimination of superfluous and awkward motions, the elaboration of correct methods of work."[34]

One hot-house of NOT in the 1920s was the Central Institute of Labor (TsIT), founded in Moscow in August 1920 by Aleksei Gastev. For Gastev and his colleagues at TsIT, the productivity of labor was considered less a matter of muscle extension than of securing the most efficient "positioning" [*ustanovka*] of the worker with regard to the specific operation being undertaken. Taking up Taylor's interest in "the mechanics of an operation" and the Gilbreths' study of the "microelements of this operation," namely, "the motions of labor and their constituent elements," TsIT devoted itself to the study of what Gastev cheerfully describes as "an extraordinarily prosaic" operation, that of metal cutting and filing [*rubka zubilom i opilovka*].[35] Through a microscopic analysis of this simple operation, assisted by photo-cyclograms, TsIT divided it into its constituent parts, distinguishing the essential, productive movements from the extrinsic, unproductive ones that stem from poor skills, bad habits, or laziness. This exhaustive analysis constituted the "narrow base" upon which, in turn, the study of more complex operations might then be tackled. The quest for efficiency extended also to the organization of the worker's immediate environment: "rule no. 3" of Gastev's list of instructions entitled, "How you need to work" [*Kak nado rabotat'*] reads "at the work-place (machine, bench, table, floor, or soil), there must be nothing superfluous [*nichego lishnego*], so that you are not rushing about and fussing to no purpose, searching for what is needed among that which is not."[36]

Under NOT, the Vulcanic muscular heroism of the worker at the forge of Dmitrii Moor's "The first of May is the All-Russian *Subbotnik*," (1920, no. 10) is superseded by the diligent *bench*-dedicated worker, demonstrated in, for example, the close-up of a young woman absorbed in the mechanics of a vise in the Ignatovichs' 1931 poster advocating communist education: "Education linked with productive work is a powerful tool in the hands of the proletariat for the creation of the new person." (no. 73) The repetition of exhortation in Mariia Bri-Bein's "Woman worker, woman collective-farm worker, behind the wheel of the tractor, at the work bench, with the rifle, be a shock-worker [*udarnitsei*] of defense," (1931, no. 100) poses a relationship of deep affinity, ease, and necessity between each operator and her respective *stanok* [bench, machine]. In other words, it is not only the *stanok* which is prosthetic in its relation to the worker, but also, equally, the worker in relation to the *stanok*. Much less in evidence in the present exhibition is abstract eulogy to the machine itself devoid of a human adjunct. (Some of the few examples of such eulogy are Natan Al'tman's postage stamp designs, the pages from the magazine *Daesh'*, and the Stenberg brothers' poster for Vertov's film "The Eleventh" [*Odinatsatyi*].)

73

100

In the third year of the Institute's operation, Gastev set out an extended defense of TsIT's interpretation of the NOT project by advancing a new concept, which he calls *trudovaia ustanovka*.[37] In this phrase, *trudovaia* [labor] is an adjective which describes the kind of *ustanovka* [positioning] TsIT desires: the predisposition in the worker to orientate himself to the world in general, in terms hitherto specific to labor alone. The *trudovaia* aspect was quickly absorbed, and *ustanovka* became the buzzword of TsIT, leading to the founding in its name of a journal (*Ustanovka rabochei sily* [*Ustanovka* of the work force]) and a joint-stock company (Ustanovka). Gastev's advocacy of the concept of *ustanovka*, in the service of NOT, reunites the physical and psychological dimensions of the word, providing an example of the dialectical project of building the collective, which required not only the collective subject's physical involvement, but also its concomitant ideological engagement: the material *ustanovka* fixes the worker in a certain position, a position expedient for production, and this material fixing also perforce admits of a certain psychological fixing of that worker's consciousness. The result of this dialectical endeavor will be the worker's reproduction of himself in the ideal form of the singular collective subject. Having been attacked by other competing NOTist groups, TsIT's burden vis-à-vis its opponents in 1924 was two-fold: first, to demonstrate that it was not just preaching Taylorism pure and simple, with its heinous exploitation of the working class by a managerial elite; and secondly, to justify its principle of the "narrow base," which its detractors derided as backwardly focused on rudimentary metal-working operations, rather than on the broad perspectives opened up by modern machine methods. The concept of *ustanovka* was TsIT's answer to these criticisms.[38]

With regard to the first issue, Gastev argues that in Western scientific management, the analysis of the mechanics of laboring operations is dedicated *solely* to establishing norms (standards) for production (i.e. the amount of time required to execute a particular operation), the exclusive emphasis on which quickly "leads to its own negation" in the form of routinization and stagnation. Whereas NOT's task, as TsIT understands it, is to encourage the worker to have the initiative to continually improve the given operation, rather than being satisfied with having (merely) achieved the established norm. The West has utterly failed, Gastev claims, "to resolve the problem of how to infect [*zarazit'*] the masses with a specific set of principles which would have provided the key to the continual improvement of the operation." In contradistinction to the Western fixation with the derivation of norms, "TsIT believes that *the creation of a set of principles*, the vaccination of each worker...with a specific organizational-labor bacillus, should be the main task of those who work in the amelioration of production....This is precisely what TsIT considers *trudovoi ustanovkoi*."[39] The worker is thus presumed diseased at the outset ("the Russian worker is a bad worker compared with people in advanced countries," Lenin proclaimed in his defense of the Soviet adaptation of Taylorism[40]); and Gastev has found the cure: *ustanovka*. This is a matter of urgency. Gastev writes, "This task must be recognized as a pressing one, especially here in the Soviet Union, where an industrial democracy unknown in other countries has been established."[41]

"The principle of *ustanovka*...is to *establish a series* of gradually developing *ustanovok*, beginning with the most rudimentary movement of the person with his own hands, through a phase of the complicating of these hands with an instrument, and finally, to a complex series of combinations of the highest reflexes with the latest industrial technology."[42] Thus Gastev's response to the second criticism: *ustanovka* does not discriminate as to the kind of labor, but rather encompasses all labor from the most primitive to the most advanced. "*Ruchnoi*" [manual] is a "backward" form of labor, only if the laborer is "*ruchnoi*" in his attitude to his work. Similarly, so-called artisanal [*remeslennyi*] labor, which in the 1920s is usually synonymous with "primitive," is such, according to Gastev, only when it is organized by intuitive guesswork rather than by mathematical calculation.[43]

Ustanovka thus provides an interpretation of NOT that does not make the latter dependent upon the acquisition of modern machinery. But if Gastev is able to resist what he sees as his opponents' fetishization of the machine, it is because his entire conception of human labor is predicated upon the latter's mechanization. Three years earlier, Gastev had written: "The world of the machine, the world of mechanism...is creating its own collective bonds, is giving birth to new types of people, whom we must accept just as we accepted the machine, and not beat our heads against the gears."[44] In 1924 the concept of *ustanovka* enables Gastev to more fully theorize his earlier statement, for *ustanov*ized labor transforms the body itself into a machine: "We begin with the most primitive, with the most rudimentary movement and we produce *the mechanization of the person himself*."[45] TsIT's analysis of labor motions and body posture was to establish an incontrovertible calculation, a formula which would permit the automatization (mechanization) of the worker's body.[46] For Gastev, the "automatism of the human being is not in any contradiction whatsoever with his organic creativity": for it is precisely the complete mechanization of motions which will afford the worker the "freedom" to discover improvements to it. Thus Gastev believes he has solved the riddle of worker-initiative, of how "to activate the working masses, to inspire in them the demon of the inventor [*besa izobretatelia*]."[47]

"*We do not recognize the difference* between so-called physical labor and so-called mental labor. The very same *rubka zubilom*...gives us the key to the building of so-called mental work....*Trudovaia ustanovka*...[is] *a great chain of the switching on* [vkliucheniia] *of simple and complex reactions, the creation of powerful automata, the switching on of these automata in complexes, continually enlivening these automata with new reactions.*" Upon the basis of the prosaic operation of metal-cutting, "which in its single coordinated act takes all of three-quarters of a second, it is possible to construct a kind of mechanics of *ustanovok*...applicable...everywhere. In this way, little by little," Gastev claims, "we give birth to the machine," without even noticing: "For us the machine is organic, a directly fated requirement of our system."[48] *Ustanovka* itself thus produces the machine, a great chain of human automata, a "current" of human labor. In the process of this transformation, subjectivity is reconfigured as an excess improper to the worker; stripped of subjectivity, or rather, collapsed into the machine, the laboring subject is reconstituted as a kind of mechanical being. But the question of who in the "mechanized collective" switches on the current, once what Spengler describes as "the modern sorcerer...the switchboard with levers and labels at which the workman calls mighty effects into play by the pressure of a finger"[49] is re-composed as the collective body itself, remains unanswered in the Gastevian vision. A photomontage by El Lissitzky from the export version of *USSR in Construction*, entitled "The Current is Switched On," (1932) in which the abstract heroism of the switch replaces that of the forge, provides an unambiguous answer.

The intense one-on-one relationship between worker and machine discussed above, gives way, in the graphic imaging of the "mechanized collectivism"[50] of labor under NOT, to repetition and uniformity. In many cases, the disposition of the pictorial field along a diagonal axis mitigates the quality of stasis that repetition might otherwise imply. Even in the hands of less provocative designers, repetition is a responsive stylistic device: in Dobrokovskii's "Build industrial cooperation. Towards the common goal through the cooperative associations [*arteli*],"[51] (n.d., no. 75) the poster cuts out a mere segment of the patterning of the interminable repetition of cutters, filers, and machinists. At the bottom, the note "Handicraftsmen [*kustari*] into cooperative associations. Cooperative associations into unions [*soiuzy*]," adopts the patter of the all-inclusive system of the collective, a place within which will guarantee the artisan's continued livelihood. In Valentina Kulagina's "Women workers, women shock-workers [*udarnitsy*], strengthen the shock-brigades, master technology, increase the ranks of proletarian specialists," (1931, no. 72) the proletarian specialist, in contrast to her bourgeois counterpart, subsides into the all-pervasive rhythm of collectivized, standardized activity. Klutsis gives tremendous force to the graphic device of repetition in several large tableaux of marching coal-miners in the present exhibition such as the heroic "We will repay the coal debt to the country." (1930, no. 91)

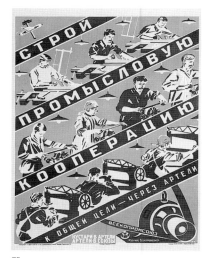

75

72

The military rhetoric which shadows the device of repetition is seen nowhere so explicitly as in Leonid Chupiatov's "Set a Bolshevik pace in preparation for the sowing," (1931, no. 88) where the formation of tractors as if they were tanks is reinforced by an explanatory note which exhorts the mass collectivization of agriculture for the liquidation of the *kulaks* as a class. (The end result of collectivization and de*kulak*ization was, in the rhetoric of Lazar Kaganovich, one of the most ruthless and bloody of Stalin's overseers of these twin policies in the Ukraine and other republics, "We were a country of the plough, we have become a country of the tractor and combine." [no. 99]) Stepanova's fly-page for Maiakovskii's "Menacing Laughter,"[52] (1932) composed of the endless repetition of a soldier with bayonet, thus returns the spectator to a fundamental source for, and result of, repetition in the graphic imaging of labor under NOT: the increasing militarization [*voenizatsiia*], throughout the course of the 1920s of the general project of the building of socialism.[53] One of the chief criticisms of Gastev's so-called "scientific method" was that its author had reductively and inappropriately based his labor research primarily upon, besides the already narrow examples provided by the metal-working industries, military models of organization. In fact, Gastev went even further, by proposing that the *ustanovochnyi metod*, derived within the context of the scientific organization of labor, be extended and applied to all aspects of life: "Even when we go out *the factory gates*, even then we carry within ourselves the productivist *ustanovku*. We are already so responsive to everything around us, that this environment becomes for us nothing other than a specific series of *ustanovok*...our *ustanovochnyi* method allows us to do only one thing—to unceasingly revolutionize everything that exists, even beyond the factory. Whether this is a matter of everyday life [*byt*], or... of *culture* in general, we will have to produce a system of *ustanovki*, of so-called cultural *ustanovki*."[54]

88

The graphic device of repetition is of course not singular to Soviet Russia. But my argument is not about exclusivity but specificity: while repetition is probably most often associated in the twentieth century with the possibilities encompassed by mechanical reproduction, it seems to me that in the early Bolshevik imagination, there is arguably a much stronger figure that prompts and shadows the device, namely, the memory of war. The Red Star, which embodies the contradictory tension that I have been tracing in this essay, between the impulse for leveling and that for the restitution of hierarchy, turns out to have been the blueprint of the collective. At the height of the Bolsheviks' obsession with delimitation and classification, with the excision of excess and difference, we get a glimpse of the tantalizing underbelly of this process, what might be called, from a position of luxury probably not affordable in the Bolshevik 1920s, genre confusion. The ultimate fate of the Soviet subject, stripped of subjectivity, militarized, collectivized, and *ustanov*ized by means of the automatic voice of the radio and the Gastevian cure, however, opens another discussion.

* My thanks to Jodi Hauptman, Karin Cope, and Golfo Alexopoulos for their suggestive and critical readings of an earlier draft of this essay.

1 See Stephen White, *The Bolshevik Poster* (New Haven: Yale University Press, 1988), 9; and Nikolai Shkolnyi, "Persuading the People: Posters of the First Soviet Years," in *Tradition and Revolution in Russian Art* (Manchester: Cornerhouse Publications, 1990), 98–107.

2 Referring to Bolshevik political posters, Nina Tumarkin writes, "The most effective depictions...were of the enemy—fat, smirking capitalists, fat, toothless priests, fat White generals in uniform." (*Lenin Lives! The Lenin Cult in Soviet Russia* [Cambridge: Harvard University Press, 1983], 72.)

3 B. C. Butnik-Siverskii, *Sovetskii plakat epokhi grazhdanskoi voiny, 1918–1921* (Moscow: Izd-vo vsesoiuznoi knizhnoi palaty, 1960), 314, entry no. 1715.

4 Richard Stites, *Revolutionary Dreams; Utopian Vision and Experimental Life in the Russian Revolution* (New York and Oxford: Oxford University Press, 1989),85.

5 The expression is Jean-Luc Nancy's with reference to Marx's analysis of the primitive "commune," see "Literary Communism," in his *The Inoperative Community*, Peter Conner et al, trans. (Minneapolis: University of Minnesota Press, 1991), 74.

6 Nikolai Tarabukin, *Iskusstvo dnia* (Moscow: Izd-vo vserossiiskii proletkul't, 1925), 32.

7 Not in this exhibition; reproduced in Alexander Lavrentiev, *Vavara Stepanova: The Complete Work*, John E. Bowlt, ed. (Cambridge: MIT Press, 1988), 147.

8 The concept of the star-as-map has its own often recited anecdote, which concerns the construction of the Theatre of the Soviet Army (1935–40) in Moscow. It is said that when Stalin was presented with plans for the building, which he refused, its architects asked what he would prefer. Taking a paper, he drew a five-pointed star; in this way, the monstrous theater came to be built upon the plan of the Red Army emblem.

9 "*Kollektiv, a, (m).* group, body; *(in many phrases does not require separate translation)*," *The Oxford Russian-English Dictionary*, Marcus Wheeler, ed. (Oxford and New York: Oxford University Press, 1984).

10 This *idée fixe* is everywhere in evidence, from the laboratory work of the avant-garde, safely although only temporarily ensconced in the state-funded Institute of Artistic Culture (INKhUK), to the State's policies on the excision of alien class elements.

11 *Vosmoi vserossiiskii s'ezd sovetov: stenografichenskii otchet* (Moscow: Gos. izd-vo, 1921), 30; cited in Jonathan Coopersmith, *The Electrification of Russia, 1880–1926* (Ithaca: Cornell University Press, 1992), 175.

12 The work's condition has suffered, but a photograph of the recto's original state shows the striding figure of Lenin with a pylon under his right arm, a literal testimony to Lenin's advocacy of the GOELRO Plan, which was elaborated in1920, given political approval at the 8th Congress of the Soviets in December 1920, and finally ratified, in somewhat modified form, at the 9th Congress in December 1921. (A copy of the photograph is preserved in the State Museum of V.V. Maiakovskii in Moscow, Izograf Fond, *inv. no.* 11672.) On the verso of the sheet is an unfinished "dynamic city" in pencil and gouache.

13 Nikolai Aseev, "Gastev," *Sobranie sochineniia v 4-kh tomakh* vol. 1 (Moscow, 1930), 202; cited in Kendall Bailes, "Alexei Gastev and the Soviet Controversy over Taylorism, 1918–1924," *Soviet Studies* vol. 29, no. 3 (July 1977): 373.

14 D. Kozlov, "Novoe o Velemire Khlebnikove," *Krasnaia nov'* no. 8 (August 1927): 185.

15 See "Radio budushchego," [The Radio of the future] in D. Kozlov, "Novoe o Velemire Khlebnikove," op. cit.: 185–188; republished in Iu. Tynianov and N. Stepanov, eds., *Sobranie proizvedenii Velemira Khlebnikova*, 5 vols. (Leningrad: Izd-vo pisatelei, 1928–1933), vol. 4, 290–295, with an editorial note explaining the differences between the *Krasnaia nov'* version and the original manuscript, and citing in full the latter's original opening paragraphs (vol. 4, 340). A recent English translation of Khlebnikov's text is made by Paul Schmidt from the *Sobranie* volume, but without reference to

Tynianov and Stepanov's important editorial note, in Charlotte Douglas, ed., *Collected Works of Velimir Khlebnikov*, 2 vols. (Cambridge: Harvard University Press, 1987), vol. 1, 392–396.

16　On ROSTA and the "agit-windows," see the discussion in Leah Dickerman, "Building the Collective," in this catalog.

17　"Rosta budushchego," manuscript, 1921, cited by Tynianov and Stepanov in *Sobranie*, op. cit., vol. 4, 340. Unless otherwise noted, translations in this essay are my own.

18　"Radio," in *Collected Works of Velimir Khlebnikov*, Schmidt, trans., op. cit., vol. 1, 393 (slightly modified).

19　"Radio," in *Sobranie*, op. cit., vol. 4, 292.

20　Kazimir Malevich, "Nashi zadachi," *Izobrazitel'noe Iskusstvo* no. 1 (1919): 74.

21　"Radio," in *Sobranie*, op. cit., vol. 4, 293.

22　Ibid., 294–295. The Faustian character of the technological apparatus underscores Khlebnikov's vision throughout the text. According to Kozlov, Khlebnikov described Walt Whitman as a "cosmic psychoradioreceiver" [*kosmicheskim psikhopriemnikom*], part of his thesis of the poet as the "medium" of the age, who, like a radio receiver, receives and despatches the ideas, feelings, will-waves of humanity. See Kozlov, "Novoe," op. cit.: 179.

23　"Radio," in *Collected Works of Velimir Khlebnikov*, Schmidt, trans., op. cit., vol. 1, 396.

24　"Radio," in *Sobranie*, op. cit., vol. 4, 291.

25　Letter to M.A. Bonch-Bruevich, the director of the state's Radio Laboratory at Nizhnii Novgorod, 5 February 1920, first published in *Telegrafiia i telefoniia bez provodov* no. 23 (Nizhnii Novgorod: 1924); reprinted in V. I. Lenin, *Polnoe sobranie sochinenii*, vol. 51 (Moscow: Izd-vo politicheskoi literatury, 5th ed., 1965), 130.

26　Blair Ruble, "Moscow's Revolutionary Architecture and its Aftermath: A Critical Guide," in William C. Brumfield, ed., *Reshaping Russian Architecture: Western Technology, Utopian Dreams* (Washington: Woodrow Wilson International Center for Scholars, and Cambridge: Cambridge University Press, 1990), 126.

27　Ushin's photomontage maquettes for the covers of John Scott-Taggart's manuals *Radio Tube* and *Radio Antenna* (no. 36, 37) raise the interesting question of the "popular" dimension of the radio phenomenon. Scott-Taggart was a young English radio-engineer who wrote many popular "how-to" manuals in the early 1920s concerning radio transmission and reception. The preparation of Russian translations of Scott-Taggart should be understood in the context of the increasing domestication of access to radio technology. Around 1923–24 there is a marked shift from the exclusively technical orientation of journals such as *Telegrafiia i telefoniia bez provodov*, published since 1918 by the State Radio Laboratory, to the emergence of new journals with a so-called "popular-scientific approach," [*popul_arnyi-nauchnyi podkhod*] such as *Radio vsem* [Radio for everyone] and *Radioliubitel'* [Radio amateur], which reproduce photographs of young Russian families head-phoned around radio sets, comparable to those which appeared in American magazines of the same period. However, the fact of increased access does not modify the centralized creation of the "single will," since the Bolsheviks officially took control of the air-waves, and thus of broadcasting, in 1922.

28　Lewis Siegelbaum, *Soviet State and Society between Revolutions, 1918–1929* (Cambridge: Cambridge University Press, 1992), 117. With regard to this issue Jacques Derrida writes, "the very name of the USSR is the name of an etatic individual, an individual and singular state that has given itself or claimed to give itself its own proper name without reference to any singular place or any national past. At its foundation, a state has given itself a purely artificial, technical, conceptual, general, conventional, and constitutional name, a common name in sum, a 'communist' name: in short, a purely political name. I know of no other example of a comparable phenomenon in the word." ("Back from Moscow, in the USSR," in Mark Poster, ed., *Politics, Theory, and Contemporary Culture* [New York: Columbia University Press, 1993], 198–199.)

37

29   Leon Trotskii, "Radio, nauka, tekhnika i obshchestvo," *Krasnaia nov'* no. 2 (February 1927): 133–143; translated by Brian Pearce as "Radio, Science, Technology, and Society," in *Problems of Everyday Life and Other Writings on Culture and Science* (New York: Monad Press, 1973), 250, 259–260, 263.

30   "Rosta budushchego," manuscript, 1921, cited by Tynianov and Stepanov in *Sobranie*, op. cit., vol. 4, 340. It is precisely the practice of "artificial" word formation praised by Khlebnikov, that is deplored by the philologist A. M. Selishchev in his study of the impact of the revolution upon the Russian language. Selishchev likewise attributes such word formation to the incursion of telegraphic communication (especially the abbreviation of institutional addresses) upon Russian syntax and lexicon. See A. M. Selishchev, "Revoliutsiia i iazyk," *Na putiakh k pedagogicheskomu samoobrazovaniiu* no. 1 (Moscow: Mir, 1925): 214–216. Ilya Ehrenburg cites the pared-down language of the telegraph as one of the features of modern life that could provide a model for the new constructivist literature; see *A vse-taki ona vertitsiia* (Berlin Helikon, 1922), 96.

31   "Radio," in *Sobranie*, op. cit., vol. 4, 294.

32   The "counter-plans" [*vstrechnye tekhpromfinplany*] were an integral part of strenuous efforts in the early 1930s to further increase the industrial productivity of all Soviet enterprises. "Counter-plans" sought to ensure that workers would not simply meet the norms set forth in the state's Five-Year Plans, but surpass them. It was within the context of the counter-plans, Alec Nove writes, that the coal miner Aleksei Stakhanov (from whose name the term "stakhanovism" is derived) achieved output fourteen times greater than the norm, in September 1935. See Alec Nove, *An Economic History of the USSR, 1917–1991*, 3rd and final edition (London: Penguin, 1992), 235.

33   The term itself is derived from the visual graphing of economic data.

34   "The Immediate Tasks of the Soviet Government," in Robert Tucker, ed., *The Lenin Anthology* (New York: Norton & Co., 1975), 447, 448–449.

35   Aleksei Gastev, "Trudovye ustanovki," *Organizatsiia truda* no. 1 (Moscow: March 1924): 21–22 (reprinted in full in Aleksei Gastev, *Kak nado rabotat'* [Moscow: Ekonomika, 1966], 191–197). This article appears in the first number of the Institute's journal *Organizatsiia Truda* when it recommenced publication with the renewed support of the Party leadership in March 1924 after a hiatus of more than a year; it may thus be considered a statement of TsIT's new platform.

36   Aleksei Gastev, "Kak nado rabotat'," in his *Poeziia rabochego udara*, repr. 6th ed. (Moscow: Sovetskii pisatel', 1964), 270.

37   Gastev, "Trudovye ustanovki," op. cit.: 22.

38   On TsIT's opponents, especially, the so-called "Group of Communists," see Bailes, "Alexei Gastev," op. cit.: 386–391.

39   Gastev, "Trudovye ustanovki," op. cit.: 21–22 (original emphasis).

40   "Immediate Tasks," in Tucker, ed., *The Lenin Anthology*, op. cit., 448.

41   Gastev, "Trudovye ustanovki," op. cit.: 21–22 (original emphasis).

42   Ibid.: 23 (original emphasis).

43   On the foremen's resistance to NOTism in this regard, see Lewis Siegelbaum, "Masters of the Shop Floor: Foremen and Soviet Industrialization," in Lewis Siegelbaum and William Rosenberg, eds., *Social Dimensions of Soviet Industrialization* (Bloomington: Indiana University Press, 1993), 166–192.

44   "Nashi zadachi," *Organizatsiia truda* no. 1 (March 1921): 14; cited in Bailes, "Aleksei Gastev," op. cit.: 384.

45   Gastev, "Trudovye ustanovki," op. cit.: 23 (original emphasis).

46   "The less perfect the movement, the more elements of stoppage, the less motor automatism. Perfect possession of the given movement implies maximum automatism." (Gastev, "Trudovye ustanovki," op. cit.: 23 [original emphasis].)

47   Ibid.: 23–24, 25.

48   Ibid.: 24 (original emphasis). See Nikolai Tarabukin's call for the "scientific organization

of intellectual labor (NOUT)," in his "Ratsionalizatsiia umstvennogo truda," *Vremia*
no. 8 (1924): 16–20.

49   Oswald Spengler, *The Decline of the West*, 2 vols., Charles Francis Atkinson, trans.
(New York: Alfred A. Knopf, 1986), vol. 2, 500.

50   In 1919, Gastev had drawn up a taxonomy of workers, based upon an analysis of the
work-force of the machine-building industry. Of the five categories of workers ranging
from highly skilled to utterly unskilled, Gastev proposes that the third category be the
"mean," the model for a proletarian psychology which is becoming increasingly
mechanized and standardized. Manifestations of this "mechanized collectivism" are,
Gastev enthusiastically writes, "so foreign to personality, so anonymous, that the
movement of these collective complexes is similar to the movement of things, in which
there is no longer any individual face but only regular, uniform steps and faces devoid
of expression, of a soul, of lyricism, of emotion, measured not by a shout or a smile but
by a pressure gauge or a speed gauge." ("O tendentsiiakh proletarskoi kul'tury,"
Proletarskaia Kul'tura no. 9–10 [1919]: 35–45; cited in Bailes, "Aleksei Gastev,"
op. cit.: 378.)

51   An *artel* is a cooperative association, or collective, of peasants or workers.

52   Not in this exhibition; reproduced in Lavrentiev, *Vavara Stepanova*, op. cit., 133.

53   Mark von Hagen examines this concept in his "Soldiers in the Proletarian Dictatorship:
From Defending the Revolution to the Building of Socialism," in Sheila Fitzpatrick,
Alexander Rabinowitch, and Richard Stites, eds., *Russia in the Era of NEP*
(Bloomington: Indiana University Press, 1991), 156–173.

54   Gastev, "Trudovye ustanovki," op. cit.: 24–25 (original emphasis).

The plates in this catalog are organized in three historically defined groupings—works from the Civil War (1918–1921); from the period of the New Economic Policy (1921–1927); and from that of the First and Second Five-Year Plans (1928–1937). While this organization creates some artificial divisions, in general, it clarifies important patterns and shifts in representational strategies. Unless otherwise noted, all the works presented (to the best of the editor's knowledge) were created as lithographs.

CIVIL WAR 1918–1921

1
Dmitrii Moor
1919
Revvoensovet [Revolutionary-Military Council of the Republic], n. 29
Edition: 20,000
90.5 x 67.6 cm. (35 5/8 x 26 5/8 in.)

Top line:	Russian Socialist Federative Soviet Republic. Proletariat of all countries unite!
Top left corner:	Hunger.
Top left arc:	The worker forges weapons.
Top arc:	The Communist points out the enemy [represented in the poster by the figures of a capitalist, a priest, and a White guard] and leads into battle.
Top right corner:	Slavery.
Top right arc:	The peasant delivers the bread.
Mid-center:	Worker-peasant defense.
Lower left:	The woman takes the place of the fighter who has gone to the front.
Lower right:	The youth learns soldiering.
Lower center:	Soviet Russia is a camp under siege. Everyone to the defense!
At bottom:	Anyone tearing down this poster or pasting over it commits a counter-revolutionary act.

2
Aleksei Radakov
March 29, 1917
Parus [Sail]
54.3 x 55.4 cm. (21 3/8 x 21 9/16 in.)

Autocratic structure.
We rule you.
We pray for you.
We judge you.
We defend you.
We feed you.
And you work.

3
Aleksei Radakov
1920
Petrograd, Gosizdat [State Publishing House]
96 x 66 cm. (37 13/16 x 26 in.)

Large print: The illiterate person is like
                a blind man. On all sides
                failure and misfortune
                lie in wait for him.
Small print: Books: About market-
                gardening and cattle
                breeding, about pig
                breeding, soil-science,
                and about agricultural
                questions.

НЕГРАМОТНЫЙ тот-же СЛЕПОЙ
ВСЮДУ ЕГО ЖДУТ НЕУДАЧИ И НЕСЧАСТЬЯ ·

15 Государственная типография, Петроград, Звенигородская, 11.

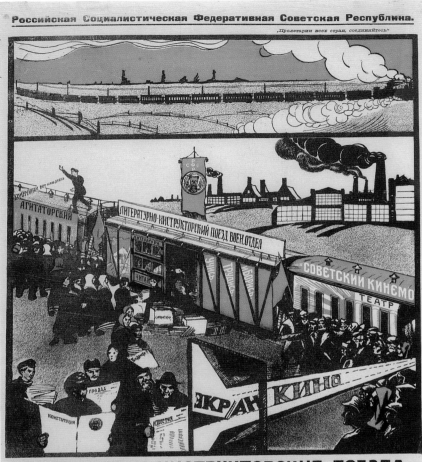

4
Anonymous
c.1920
Publishing House of the All-Russian
Executive Committee of the Soviet of
Workers', Peasants', Red Army Soldiers',
and Cossacks' Affairs
71 x 51.4 cm. (28 x 20 1/4 in.)

Left car:	"Agitational." Figure on top shouts "Communism is our motto."
Center car top:	"Literary-instructional train, military division."
Center car left:	"Read."
Center car right:	"Learn. Labor. And fight." (on pennants)
Right car:	"Soviet cinematography."
Below:	"Theater."
Beam of light:	"Cinema." "Screen."
Bottom headline:	Literary-instructional trains of the All-Russian Central Executive Committee. Our train.
Text begins:	The living, spoken word, books, pictures, theater —everything which can carry a little light into the countryside and the dark corners of Russia—that is what the literary instructional train carries....

(Starting in 1919, as part of an effort to win the allegiance of provincial populations, the Bolsheviks sent decorated trains— called "agit-trains"—out from the center. The trains carried activists, pamphlets, and often, cinematic equipment.)

5
S.A.
Glavlit [Main Administration for Literary Publications under the Commissariat of Enlightenment]
Edition: 5,000
35.2 x 53 cm. (13⅞ x 20⅞ in.)

Earlier I was an oiler, I oiled the wheels. And now I'm in the Soviet. I decide issues.

6
Dmitrii Moor
1920
Moscow Revvoensovet [Revolutionary-Military Council of the Republic], n. 79
10.9 x 12.3 cm. (27 11/16 x 31 1/4 in.)

Peoples of the Caucasus!
The Tsars and generals, the landlords and capitalists have suppressed your freedom by gun and sword and sold your country to the bankers of many lands. The Red Army of Soviet Russia has conquered your enemies, it has brought you liberation from servitude of the rich. Long live Soviet Caucasia!

(In Russian, Amenian, Georgian, Ottoman, Turkish, and Tatar.)

7
Natan Al'tman
Pen and ink
22.9 x 18.1 cm. (9 x 7 1/8 in.)

RSFSR Post

(RSFSR was the acronym for the Russian Soviet Federal Socialist Republic.)

8
Natan Al'tman
Pen and ink
22.9 x 18.1 cm. (9 x 7 1/8 in.)

RSFSR Post

9
Natan Al'tman
Pen and ink
26.4 x 17.9 cm. (10 3/8 x 7 1/16 in.)

RSFSR Post

at right:
10
Dmitrii Moor
1920
Moscow Revvoensovet [Revolutionary-Military Council of the Republic], n. 81
73.2 x 52.7 cm. (28 13/16 x 20 3/4 in.)

Top line: Proletariat of all countries
                  unite!
Bottom: The first of May is the
                  All-Russian *Subbotnik.*

(The Subbotnik *was voluntary Saturday* [subbota] *labor for the state.)*

11
Viktor Deni
Autumn 1919
Revvoensovet [Revolutionary-Military Council of the Republic], n. 48
Edition: 113, 500
107.5 x 70.6 cm. (425/16 x 2713/16 in.)

Above:	Denikin's Band.
Flag:	"Beat the workers and the peasants."
Below:	Defend the Soviets. Defend your will, your power. Address to the peasants by Dem'ian Bednyi [a poet].
Bottom:	Anyone tearing down this poster or pasting over it commits a counter-revolutionary act.

(Anton Denikin was the general of one of the White armies challenging the Bolsheviks, or Reds.)

12
Viktor Deni
1920
Revvoensovet [Revolutionary-Military Council of the Republic], n. 30
98.1 x 75.6 cm. (385/8 x 293/4 in.)

Top:	League of Nations.
Top left:	Proletariat of all nations unite!
On flag:	Capitalists of all nations unite!
Bottom:	Anyone tearing this poster or pasting over it commits a counter-revolutionary act.

13
Viktor Deni
1920
Political Department of the Reserve Army of the Republic and the
Procurator of the Baltic
62 x 49 cm. (21 1/8 x 19 1/8 in.)

Below head: "Capital."
On knife: "Communism."
Bottom: The last hour!

14
Viktor Deni
1921
Petrograd, Gosizdat [State Publishing House]
Edition: 5,000
43.7 x 35.9 cm. (17 3/16 x 14 1/8 in.)

3rd internation[al].

*(Also called the Communist International or Comintern, the Third
International was an international organization of European socialist
parties dedicated to the transformation of the Russian Revolution
into a pan-European Revolution.)*

15a
Dmitrii Moor
c.1920
Gouache maquette
60.6 x 49.2 cm. (23⅞ x 19⅜ in.)

See no. 15b

15b
Dmitrii Moor
1920
Moscow Revvoensovet [Revolutionary-Military Council of the Republic], n. 83
70.6 x 53.6 cm. (28 x 21 in.)

The Soviet Turnip.

First level: Monsieur Capital looks at the turnip. "I'll pull it out without anyone noticing." He tugs it this way and that; he pulls and pulls, but cannot pull it out.
Small sign: The local inhabitants.
Second level: Grandpa-Capital dreams evil thoughts and pulls. Grandma he calls a "Counter-Revolutionary."
Third level: "We will give the turnip a good thrashing," yelled Grandma, calling her helper—her granddaughter.
In figure's skirts: Social-compromiser.
Fourth level: Grandpa, Grandma, and Grandaughter were straining themselves. At the rear, the faithful bitch is trying as well.
In dog's skirts: The bitch-saboteur.
Fifth level: Everyone flew, crashing hard; the Soviet Turnip punished all. That's what you get for trying to pull out a turnip.

Великий буржуаз-
ный ученый,
Великий путешес-
твенник Нансен
Буржуев угова-
ривая долго, „помоги-
те“-

Голодают русские
крестьяне.
Вымирает Волга.“

Совещались бур-
жуи в Женеве,
Совещались в
Брюсселе,

„Помочь не можем.

А требуем призна-
ния царского дол-
га“

А в это время от
хлеба ломится Ка-
нада:
В ней гниет хлеба
в три раза боль-
ше, чем
для прокормления
Поволжья надо.

Вместо того, чтоб
спасти
25000000 кресть-
ян,
На Волгу напра-
вить хлебные
грузы,

В Аргентине, бур-
жуи.
Паровозы топят
пудами кукурузы.

Помни-же, голод-
ный,
Помни, красноар-
меец,
Помни рабоче-
крестьянская
рать!-

Тот, кто имел все,
для спасенья-

25.000.000.

Дает
25000000 голод-
ных умирать

С ним один разго-
вор
Вот:
Пальцы за глотку
Коленом в живот

16
Ivan Maliutin
GPP [Glavpolitprosvet], n. 392
October 1921
Stencilled gouache
12 frames, each approx. 55 x 41 cm. (approx. 21 x 16 in.)

1. Great bourgeois scholar, great traveler Nansen long attempted to persuade the bourgeois: "Help.
2. Russian peasants are starving. The Volga is dying."
3. The bourgeois deliberated in Geneva, deliberated in Brussels.
4. "We cannot help.
5. But we demand recognition of the tsarist debt."
6. And at this time Canada is bursting with wheat. Three times as much wheat rots [there] as is needed to feed the people of the Volga.
7. Instead, send cargoes of wheat to the Volga in order to save 25,000,000 peasants.
8. In Argentina, the bourgeois drown locomotives with pounds of corn.
9. Remember, hungry man; remember, Red Army soldier; remember, worker-peasant masses!
10. That he who had everything for their salvation
11. Let 25,000,000 starving people die.
12. To him, there is only one thing to say: "Fingers on the throat, knee in the gut!"

(Deaths from hunger and disease in the years 1920 and 1921 exceeded the combined total of Russian casualties from World War I and the Civil War.)

(Glavpolitprosvet, the political education department of the Commissariat of Enlightenment, took over the administration of the poster-making collaborative in January 1921. ROSTA posters made in this later period are marked by the initials "GPP," followed by a number.)

17
Vladimir Kozlinskii
1920 or 1921
Linocut
Petrograd ROSTA
71.4 x 49.8 cm. (28 1/8 x 19 5/8 in.)

Despite the efforts of enemies throughout
the world over the last three years, the
Revolution proceeds by giant strides!

18
Vladimir Kozlinskii
1921
Linocut
Petrograd ROSTA
66.1 x 41.9 cm. (26 1/16 x16 1/2 in.)

Work and there will be flour. Sit with
crossed arms and there will not be flour
[*muká*] but suffering [*múka*].

19
Vladimir Kozlinskii
1921
Linocut
Petrograd ROSTA
77.8 x 46.2 cm. (30 5/8 x 18 3/16 in.)

The dead of the Paris Commune have
risen under the red banner of the Soviets!

at right:
20
Vladimir Kozlinskii
1921
Linocut
Petrograd ROSTA
62.2 x 34.3 cm. (24 1/2 x 13 1/2 in.)

The Kronstadt card is beaten!

*(See "Building the Collective," pages
20–21, for a discussion of Kronstadt.)*

КРОНШТАДТСКАЯ!

ПЕТЕРБУРГ   РОСТА-

КАРТА БИТА!

at left, top:
21
Anonymous
c.1920
Smolensk ROSTA
23.7 x 46 cm. (9 9/16 x 18 1/8 in.)

Upper right:	Proletariat of all nations unite!
Main text:	Organization of production is victory over the capitalistic regime.

at left, bottom:
22
Anonymous
c.1920
Political Directorate of the Western Front, n. 13
Commission of the Red Gift under the Political Directorate of the Western Front
26.5 x 58.7 cm. (10 7/16 x 23 1/8 in.)

Organize "Red Gift Week" here and everywhere.

23
Wladyslaw Strzeminski (?)
c.1920
Smol[ensk] ROSTA
72.7 x 44.9 cm. (28 5/8 x 17 11/16 in.)

Top:	The Red Army heroically guards the front. The Red rear [the home front] must help the Red front.
Top left:	Worker—you must redouble production.
Top right:	Peasant—you must yield twice as much product as allotted.
Small sign:	Bread.
Mid-left:	Railwayman—increase the repair of locomotives and railway cars.
Mid-right:	And you—the rest of the citizens —send gifts to the soldiers at the front.

24
Vladimir Lebedev
c.1920
Gouache and ink
26.7 x 21.7 cm. (10 1/2 x 8 5/16 in.)

The union of the country and the city, the workers, and the peasants.

25
Gustav Klutsis
1920
Photomontage maquette
46.3 x 27.5 cm. (18 1/4 x 10 13/16 in.)

The electrification of the entire country

*(A photograph of the photomontage's original state, preserved in the
State Museum of V.V. Maiakovskii [Izograf Fond, inv. no. 11672],
shows the striding figure of Lenin with a pylon under his right arm—
a literal testimony to Lenin's advocacy of the GOELRO [State
Commission for the Electrification of Russia] Plan, which was elaborated in 1920 and given political approval in December of the same
year. The Plan was to ensure the "electrification of the entire country.")*

NEP 1921–1927

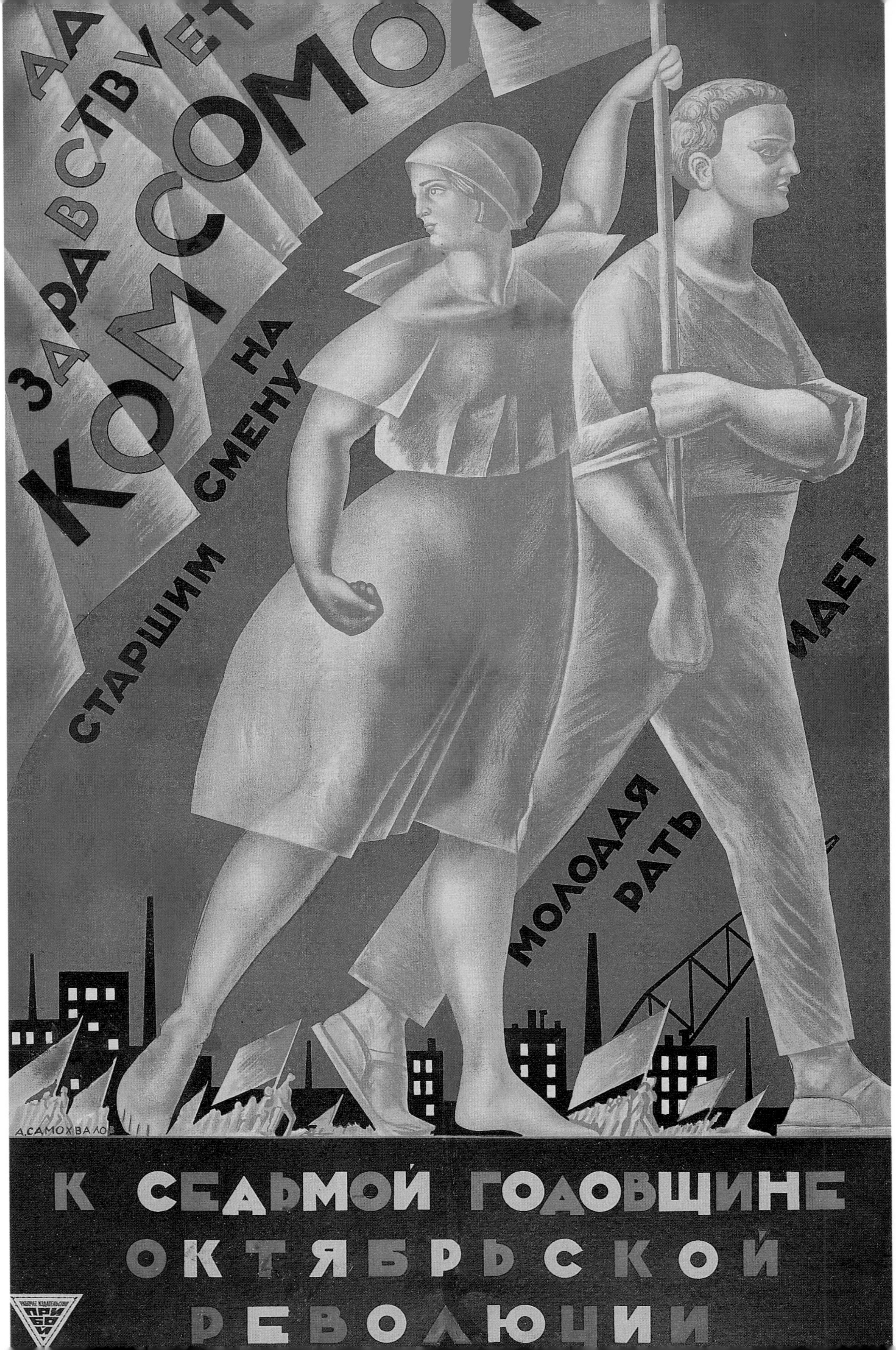

ДА ЗДРАВСТВУЕТ КОМСОМОЛ

НА СМЕНУ СТАРШИМ

МОЛОДАЯ РАТЬ ИДЕТ

А. САМОХВАЛОВ

К СЕДЬМОЙ ГОДОВЩИНЕ
ОКТЯБРЬСКОЙ
РЕВОЛЮЦИИ

26
Aleksandr Samokhvalov
1924
Priboi [Surf], Leningrad
Edition: 5000
89.9 x 60 cm. (35 3/8 x 23 5/8 in.)

Long live the *Komsomol* [the Communist League of Youth]. Young
forces are coming to relieve their seniors. In honor of the seventh
anniversary of the October Revolution.

27
Gustav Klutsis
Sergei Sen'kin
1927
Photomontage maquette for book cover
38.1 x 58.4 cm. (15 x 23 in.)

To the memory of dead leaders.

28
Adolf Strakhov
1924
Mistetstvo
Edition: 30,000
93.8 x 65.4 cm. (365/16 x 253/4 in.)

1870–1924
V. Ul'ianov (Lenin)

(Lenin died in 1924. After a fierce power struggle among members of the Party's Politburo, Joseph Stalin acceded to power.)

29
Aleksandr Rodchenko
1925
MGSPS [Moscow City Council of Professional Unions]
"Labor and Book"
Edition: 10,000
35.7 x 25.7 cm. (14 1/16 x 10 1/8 in.)

The worker alone is weak. The professional union is a defense
against the proprietor's clutches.

30
Aleksandr Rodchenko
1925
MGSPS [Moscow City Council of Professional Unions]
"Labor and Book"
Edition: 10,000
25.2 x 35.2 cm. (9 5/16 x 13 7/8 in.)

I am a member of the union. The union will take care that I don't
become unemployed.

31
Yulian Shutskii
1925
Kubuch [Commission for the Improvement of Daily Life of
Schoolchildren]
Edition: 5,000
93.5 x 62.2 cm. (363/4 x 241/2 in.)

Radio. From the will of millions we will create a single will.

following pages:
32
Georgii and Vladimir Stenberg
1928
VUFKU [All-Ukrainian Film and Photography Administration]
Edition: 10,000
approx. 107 x. 71 cm. (approx. 421/8 x. 28 in.)

Center: The Eleventh.
Side: Author-Director Dziga Vertov. Chief Cameraman Kaufman.
Signed: 2 Stenberg 2.

*(The title "The Eleventh" refers to the eleventh anniversary of the
October Revolution.)*

33
Aleksandr Rodchenko
1924
Goskino [State Committee of the Council of Ministers on Cinematography]
Edition: 8,000
90.8 x 68.0 cm. (353/4 x 263/4 in.)

Top: Goskino Production Goskino.
Small emblem: Central Government Photo-Cinematic Enterprise, Moscow.
Center: Kino-Eye [*Kino-Glaz*].
Bottom: Six reels. Cameraman Kaufman. The work of Dziga Vertov.

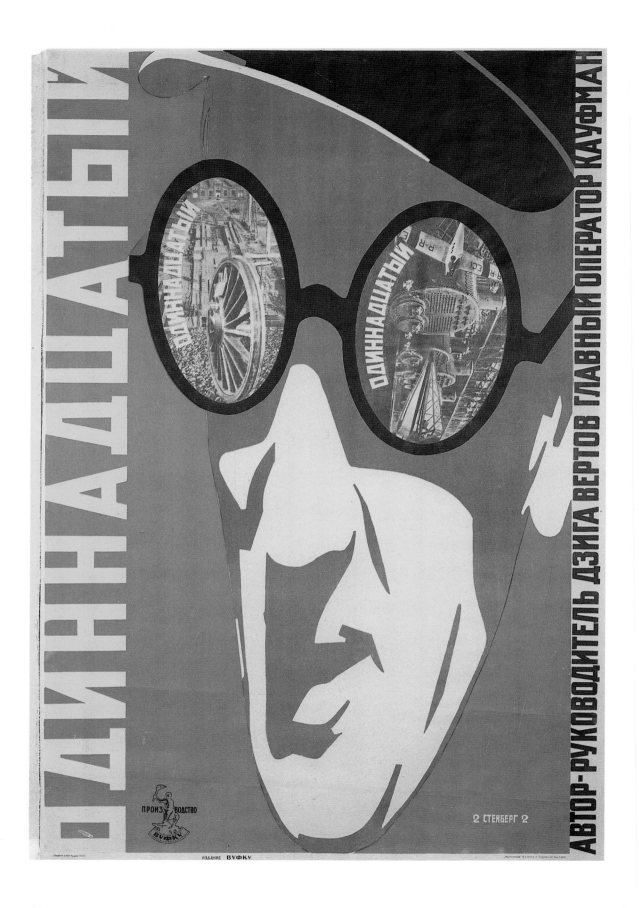

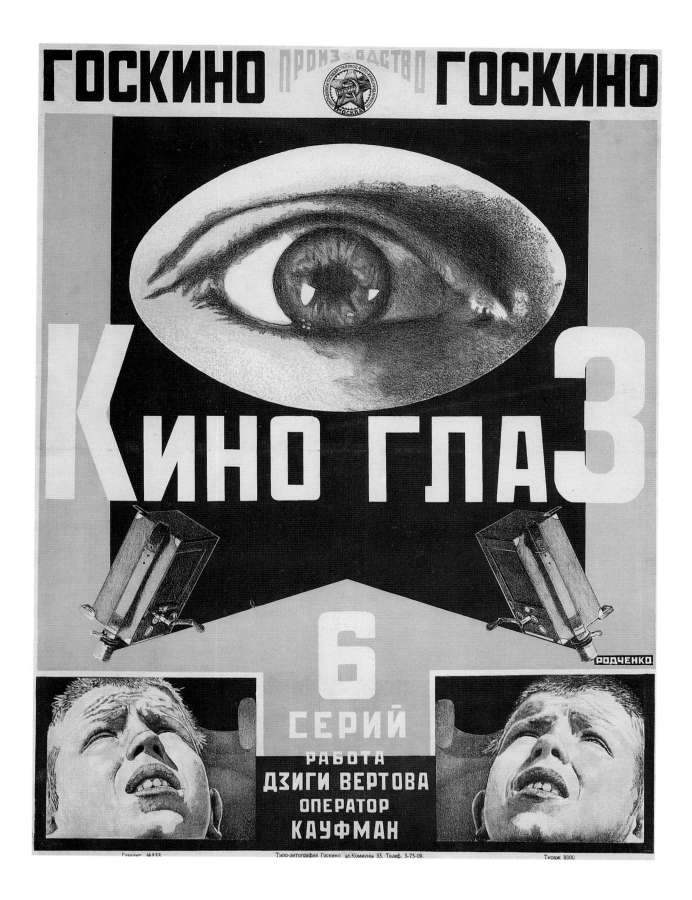

at left:
34
Georgii and Vladimir Stenberg
1928
Sovkino [All-Russian Photographic
and Cinematic Joint-Stock Company
"Soviet Film"]
Edition: 22,000
108 x 70.5 cm. (42 1/2 x 27 3/4 in.)

Bottom: Symphony of the Big City.
Side: Director—Val'ter [Walter]
Ruttman. Cameramen:
Reimer Kuntse, Robert
Babeske, L. Sheffer.
Screenplay by Carl Freund.
Sovkino Release.
2 Stenberg 2

above:
35
Elena Semenova
1926
AVIAKhIM [Society for Aid to Defense and
Aviation and Chemical Construction in the
USSR]
70.2 x 107.7 cm. (27 5/8 x 42 7/16 in.)

Left: AVIAKhIM—the support
of labor world-wide.
Right: Anti-gas aerial sentry of
the USSR.
Left quadrant: Turn to the countryside.
Right: The border of the USSR.

(AVIAKhIM was a mass quasi-voluntary
defense organization connected to the
aviation and chemical industries.)

following pages:
36, 37
Ushin
Photomontage maquettes
each 18 x 14.3 cm. (7 1/8 x 5 5/8 in.)

Scott-Taggart. *Radio Tube.*

The Radio Antenna and How to Build it.

(John Scott-Taggart was a young English
radio engineer who wrote many popular
"how-to" manuals in the early 1920s concerning radio transmission and reception.)

РАДИО

И КАК ЕЕ ПОСТРОИТЬ

АНТЕННА

above:
39
Vladimir Roskin
1925–26
Gouache maquette
21.5 x 28.4 cm. (8$\frac{1}{2}$ x 11$\frac{3}{16}$ in.)

GET

(GET is the acronym for the State Electro-Technical Trust.)

at left:
38
Vladimir Roskin
1925–26
Gouache maquette
34.3 x 25.4 cm. (13$\frac{1}{2}$ x 10 in.)

NIZHGUBSOVNARKHOZ at market in 1925.

(NIZHGUBSOVNARKHOZ is the acronym for the Nizhnyi Novgorod district branch of the Sovnarkhoz—the Commissariat of the National Economy.)

ВСЕМ... ВСЕ

ОДИН РУБЛЬ ЗОЛОТОМ
ДЕЛАЕТ КАЖДОГО
АКЦИОНЕРОМ ДОБРОЛЕТА

ДОБРОЛЕТ

ГУБЛИТ № 1069. МОСКВА.   ТИПОЛИТОГРАФИЯ ВОЗДУШНОГО ФЛОТА, Бол. Садовая, 3

40
Aleksandr Rodchenko
1923
Gublit [Regional Department for Literary and Publishing Affairs]
34.9 x 45.5 cm. (13 3/4 x 17 15/16 in.)

Top:	Everyone...Everyone...Everyone....
Right:	He who is not a stock-holder of Dobrolet is not a citizen of the USSR.
On airplane:	Dobrolet.
Below airplane:	One gold ruble makes any-one a stockholder of Dobrolet.
Bottom:	Dobrolet—sale of stock at Dobrolet and Prombank (Moscow, Stock Place [Birzhevaia pl.] 2/7 and their branches).
Signed at right:	Advertising Constructor Rodchenko Tel. 37-40.

(Dobrolet, the name of the airline, means "good flight.")

41
Aleksandr Rodchenko
1923–24
State Confectionary Factory "Red October"
25.7 x 28 cm. (10 1/8 x 11 1/16 in.)

"Red Aviator" Cookies.

Scatter among the bushes,
Enemy cavalry.
Here and everywhere
The "Aviator" pursues you.

Go crawl growling under the table.
Our aviation
Will rise above
Generals of nations.

We are propagating the idea everywhere
Even on the subject of sweets.
Our will shall triumph.
The enemy will crawl away like a crab.

(Translation by Hilde Hoogenboom.)

42a
Aleksandr Rodchenko
Text by Vladimir Maiakovskii
1923
(reconstructed by Vavara Stepanova, 1930)
Gouache over photograph
11.1 x 27.5 cm. (4 3/8 x 10 13/16 in.)

Chervonets cigarettes are good to the taste.
Strong, as strong as pure gold currency.
Nowhere else like in Mossel'prom.

(The chervonets *was a Soviet bank
note, named after a pre-revolutionary
gold coin, which was convertible to
hard currency.)*

42b
Aleksandr Rodchenko
Text by Vladimir Maiakovskii
1923
21.3 x 9.5 cm. (8 3/8 x 3 3/4 in.)

All smokers, always and everywhere, show
a preference for Red Star. Nowhere else
like in Mossel'prom.

42c
Aleksandr Rodchenko
Text by Vladimir Maiakovskii
1923
(reconstructed by Vavara Stepanova, 1930)
Gouache over photograph
8.3 x 2.1 cm. (3 1/4 x 8 1/4 in.)

All that remains with us from the old world
are Ira cigarettes. Nowhere else like in
Mossel'prom.

*(Mossel'prom was the acronym for the
Moscow Union of Industrial Enterprises
for the Processing of Agricultural Produce,
a centralized state enterprise for the
sale of agricultural products. The poet-
designer Vladimir Maiakovskii solicited
the collaboration of constructivist artists
to produce advertising which would
aid Mossel'prom in competition with
private traders.)*

43
Aleksandr Rodchenko
1924
32.1 x 23.3 (12 5/8 x 9 3/16)

Mossel'prom. Cinema Cigarettes.
25 items.

44
Anonymous
North-Caucasus Tobacco Trust. Don
Government Tobacco
21.3 x 13 cm. (8 3/8 x 5 1/8 in.)

Hammer [Cigarettes].

ТОВАРИЩИ
НЕ СПОРЬТЕ!
СОВЕТСКИЕ ГРАЖДАНЕ
ОКРЕПНУТ В СПОРТЕ
РСФСР
ЧАЕУПРАВЛЕНИЕ
МОСКВА
МЯСНИЦКАЯ 19.
ЛЕГКОРАСТВОРИМ
КАКАО
ГОЛЛАНДСКИЙ
СОБСТВЕННОЙ
ФАБРИКИ
ЧИСТЫЙ ВЕС
200ГР.
МАЯКОВСКИЙ
РОДЧЕНКО
В НАШЕЙ СИЛЕ
НАШЕ ПРАВО
В ЧЕМ СИЛА?
В ЭТОМ
КАКАО

at left:
45
Aleksandr Rodchenko
Text by Vladimir Maiakovskii
Gouache maquette
84.1 x 59.7 cm. (33 1/8 x 23 1/2 in.)

Comrades, don't argue!
Soviet citizens will become stronger in sport.
In our might is our right.
And where is this strength?
In this cocoa.

above:
46a, b
Aleksandr Rodchenko
Text by Vladimir Maiakovskii
1924
State Confectionary Factory "Red October"
each 8.2 x 7.7 cm. (3 1/4 x 3 in.)

"Our Industry" candy wrappers
"Elevator":
In springtime, the earth is black,
fluffed up just like cotton-wool.
Grain elevator, give larger seed
to the ploughed field.

"Bridge":
Don't stand by the river until old age.
It's better to throw a bridge over the river.

47a
Aleksandr Rodchenko
1923
Gouache maquette
83.8 x 50.8 cm. (33 x 20 in.)

See no. 47b

47b
Aleksandr Rodchenko
1923
Edition: 500
67.8 x 49.5 cm. (2611/16 x 191/2 in.)

Top left: Cooking oil. Attention working masses.
Top right: Three times cheaper than dairy butter! More nutritious
               than other oils!
Bottom: Nowhere else like in Mossel'prom!

СТОЛОВОЕ
МАСЛО
— ВНИМАНИЕ —
РАБОЧИХ МАСС

ВТРОЕ
ДЕШЕВЛЕ!
КОРОВЬЕГО!
ПИТАТЕЛЬНЕЕ!
ПРОЧИХ МАСЛ!

МАЯКОВСКИЙ
РОДЧЕНКО

НЕТ
НИГДЕ
КРОМЕ

КАК
В
МОССЕЛЬПРОМЕ

Моск. Гублит № 2648.

Тираж 500.

Москва, Типо-Литография МОССЕЛЬПРОМА, ул. Карла Маркса, д. 20.

48
Anonymous
Central Military Newspaper *Red Star*
106.7 x 96.5 cm. (42 x 38 in.)

Uppermost:	For the struggle for the workers' cause—Be prepared.
Top:	I, a young pioneer of the USSR, in the presence of my comrades, do solemnly swear that: 1. I will stand firmly for the working-class cause in its struggle for the emancipation of the workers and peasants of the whole world. 2. I will honestly and steadfastly carry out [Vladimir] Il'ich [Lenin]'s ordinances, and follow the laws and customs of the Young Pioneers.
First law:	The Pioneer is faithful to the affairs of the working class and the wishes [*zavety*] of Il'ich.
Second law:	The Pioneer is the younger brother and the helper of the Young Communist [Komsomolets] and the Communist.
Third law:	The Pioneer is a comrade to Pioneers, working-class and peasant children of the whole world.
Fourth law:	The Pioneer organizes surrounding children and participates with them in all surrounding life. The Pioneer is the first of all children.
Fifth law:	The Pioneer strives for knowledge. Knowledge and know-how are forces in the battle for workers' affairs.
First custom:	The Pioneer guards his health and that of others; he is hale and hearty.
Second custom:	The Pioneer values his and others' time. He does things quickly and neatly.
Third custom:	The Pioneer is hard-working and persistant, knows how to work collectively under any conditions, and finds a way around all obstacles.
Fourth custom:	The Pioneer is careful with public property, handles books, clothes, and things belonging to the workshop neatly.
Fifth custom:	The Pioneer does not swear, smoke, or drink.
Lower middle:	A changing of the guard is coming. Be prepared.
Bottom:	You must be the first builders of Communist society among millions of builders, which every young man, every young girl should be. —N[ikolai] Lenin. ("Nikolai Lenin" was an early pseudonym for the man who became Vladimir Ilyich Lenin.)

(The Pioneers were the Communist youth organization for younger children. Based in many ways on the model of the Boy Scouts, they took for themselves the motto "Be prepared.")

50
Vavara Stepanova
Text by Vladimir Maiakovskii
Gosizdat [State Publishing House]
Edition: 10,000
102.6 x 70.2 cm. (40 3/8 x 27 5/8 in.)

Peasant economy will improve with literacy. Teach children with textbooks from Gosizdat.

(Open book shows Gosizdat logo at left and a village reading room [izba], labelled "School for peasant youth," at right.)

at left:
49
Gustav Klutsis, Sergei Sen'kin
Department of Agitation and Propaganda of the Moscow Committee of the All-Russian Communist Party
Edition: 5,000
71.1 x 52.4 cm. (28 x 20 5/8 in.)

Upper right:	Activists.
Upper left:	An instructional letter on summer study for the self-taught.
Center:	Use summer for study.
Lower left:	Study.
Bottom:	Seek advice with the political cell.

51
Aleksei Levin
Text by Vladimir Maiakovskii
c.1925
Ogiz [Association of State Publishing Houses]
Edition: 6,000
107.3 x 70.4 cm. (42 1/4 x 27 3/4 in.)

Top:	Each newcomer is parched with spiritual thirst.
On books:	Belle-lettres. Village reading room. Textbooks. Library. "Peasant's Companion." Popular scientific library.
Bottom:	In the State Publishing House Store, you will instantly find any textbook, any book.

52
Natan Al'tman
1923
Gouache maquette
Priboi [Surf], Petrograd
39.2 x 29 cm. (153/8 x 117/16 in.)

Red Student no. 8 (1923)

at right:
54
Georgii and Vladimir Stenberg
1926
Izvestii TsIK SSSR [Newspaper *Izvestiia* (News) of the Central Executive Committee of the USSR]
Edition: 25,000
69.2 x 52.1 cm. (271/4 x 209/16 in.)

Subscription is opened for 1927 for the monthly literary-artistic journal *Novyi Mir* [New World].

53
Aleksei Levin
Text by Vladimir Maiakovskii
1925
Mosgublit [Moscow Regional Department for Literary and Publishing Affairs]
Edition: 15,000
106.4 x 71.1 cm. (417/8 x 277/8 in.)

Top: Workers, what do you read? Of course, the newspaper *Working Moscow*.
Bottom: Subscription is opened for the year 1925 year. Every worker, every factory—rush to subscribe.
Poem below: *(rhyming in Russian)*
         Both you and your children will find out everything on earth from the supplements of our newspaper.
         Worker, remember this: *Working Moscow* is your newspaper!
         Subscribe, and your aquaintances and close ones will quickly subscribe as well.
         The larger the print run, the closer to the masses, and the lower the price of the newspaper.
         It's guaranteed that there is and will be no delay. *Working Moscow* is delivered at first light.
         The price is cheap. The poorest person can set up a subscription on his earnings.
         Send an order, or come yourself.

55
Vladimir Stenberg
1928
Gouache and pencil
21.6 x 35.6 cm. (8 1/2 x 14 in.)

Design for *Children's Games*.

56a–f
Gustav Klutsis
1928
each approx. 15.2 x 11.4 cm.
(approx. 6 x 4 1/2 in.)

All:	Moscow Spartikada. 1928.
Tennis players:	Soviet physical culture is one of the components of the cultural revolution in the USSR.
Shot putters:	Our athletic greetings to the working-class sportsmen of the whole world.
Sharp shooters:	Every amateur athlete [*fizkul'turnik*] must be a good shot.
Runners:	For the unity of working-class sportsmen of the whole world.

(Held the same year as the Olympic Games in Amsterdam, the Spartikada was intended as a specifically proletarian athletic competition. Members of foreign Communist Party organizations, labor unions, and labor associations were invited to compete with Soviet teams.)

КОМНАТА ОТДЫХА В

57
Elena Semenova
1926
Pen, ink, and gouache
24.1 x 38.7 cm. (9$1/2$ x 15$1/4$ in.)

Relaxation room in workers' club.
Sign at right: "Showers and...."

FIVE-YEAR PLANS

1928–1937

58
Gustav Klutsis
1929
Photomontage maquette
48.5 x 35 cm. (18⅞ x 13 11/16 in.)

Plan for Socialist Offensive in 1929–30. Scheduled figures for the second year of the Five-Year Plan.
According to the State Plan, presented for the confirmation of SNK [Council of People's Commissars] and STO SSSR [Council of Labor and Defense of the USSR].

clockwise from top left:
59
Gustav Klutsis
1930
Ogiz [Association of State Publishing Houses]
Edition: 30,000
72.7 x 51.3 cm. (285/8 x 203/16 in.)

Communism is Soviet power plus electrification.
Top left: Achievements of the first year of the Five-Year Plan
               and scheduled figures for 1929–30.
Middle left: Reserves [*fondy*] of electricity: 1.3 billion 2.1 billion
Lower left: Rate of growth of the reserves: 141.9 157.0

60
Iakov Guminer
Izogiz [Leningrad State Publishing House for Art]
Edition: 15,000
72.1 x 58.9 cm. (283/8 x 211/4 in.)

Top: Arithmetic of the Counter-Plan.
Bottom: 2+2 plus the enthusiasm of workers=5.

*("Counter-Plans" sought to ensure that workers would surpass
rather than simply meet the norms set forth in the Five-Year Plans.)*

61
Gustav Klutsis
1930
Gosizdat [State Publishing House]
Edition: 30,000
105.1 x 73.7 cm. (413/8 x 29 in.)

Top: We will turn the Five-Year Plan into a Four-Year Plan with
               the efforts of millions of workers involved in socialist
               competition. The achievements of the first year of the
               Five-Year Plan and the scheduled figures for 1929/30.
Left: To raise productivity of labor 25%
               All hired labor: in 1928/29—12.2 million people;
               in 1929/30—13.3 million people
               To lower manufacturing costs 11%
               To raise worker's real wages an average of 12%
               From shock-work [*udarnie*] brigades to shock-work
               factory units.
Bottom: We will turn the Five-Year Plan into a Four-Year one.

62
Sergei Sen'kin
1931
Ogiz-Izogiz [Combined State Publishing Houses]
Edition: 30, 000
102.9 x 70.8 cm. (401/2 x 277/8 in.)

Top: We will take up the initiative of the shock-workers
               [*udarniki*]. We will give three weeks' earnings as a loan
               for the output of the third decisive year of the
               Five-Year Plan.
Center right: Fulfill the plan with the development of competition
               and shock-work [*udarnichestva*]. 100% participation.
On red bars: Increase the tempo of socialist industry! In the third
               decisive year of the Five-Year Plan, start up 518 new
               enterprises, build 1040 M.T.S [Machine Tractor Stations]!

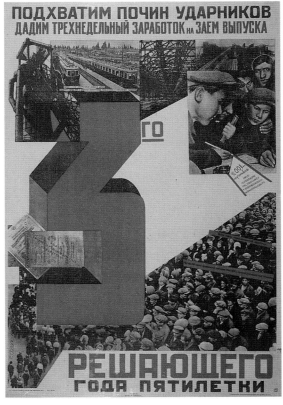

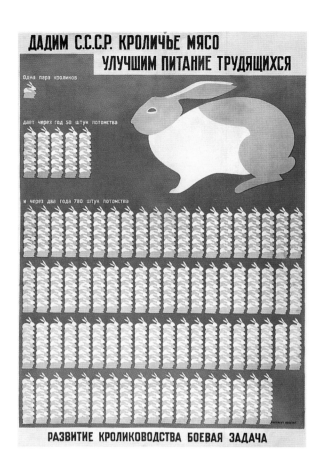

63
Anonymous
Institut izostat [Institute for the Representation of Statistics]
107 x 70.2 cm. (42 1/16 x 27 9/16 in.)

Top:	We will give the USSR rabbit meat. We will improve the workers' diet.
Center:	One pair of rabbits produces 50 descendants after one year. And after 2 years—780 descendants.
Bottom:	The development of rabbit breeding is an urgent task.

64
Nikolai Troshin
1931
State Scientific-Technical Publishing House
Edition: 11,000
72.1 x 50.5 cm. (28 3/8 x 19 7/8 in.)

Left (vertical): Lumber Production
Center: We will fulfill the Five-Year Plan in three years.
Graph: The Five-Year Plan in millions of cubo-meters.
1928/29 – 12 1929/30 – 15 1932 – 31
1928/29 – 12 1929/30 – 17 1931 – 30. 5 are expected.

(The bottom set of numbers gives the target figures for completing the Plan in three years.)

at left:
65
Mechislav Dobrokovskii
1930
104.4 x 71.44 cm. (41 x 28 1/8 in.)

Za rubezhom [Abroad]
New popular illustrated journal, dedicated to the politics, economics, and art of foreign countries.

above:
66
Aleksandr Deineka
1931
Izogiz [State Publishing House for Art]
Edition: 5,000
104 x 144.6 cm (57 x 82 1/2 in.)

Let's transform Moscow into a model socialist city of the proletarian state.

above:
67
Anonymous
Gosizdat [State Publishing House]
Edition: 3,000
68.7 x 99.1 cm. (27 1/16 x 39 in.)

Top left:	The workers of the whole world are our friends.
Top right:	The Red Army and workers are one family.
Top:	A tight bond with workers secures the power of the Red Army.
Lower:	Tsarist and bourgeois armies are implements in the hands of Capital for the oppression of workers.

at right:
68
Anonymous
The Military Herald
Edition: 10,000
98.7 x 69.4 cm. (38 7/8 x 27 5/16 in.)

Top:	The Red Army is the fighting school of the workers.
Bottom:	The Red Army learns to fight and conquer.

69
Anonymous
Central Committee of the Union of Food Workers
Edition: 7,000
103.5 x 72.7 cm. (40 3/4 x 28 3/4 in.)

Top: We are not those who are frightened by
                difficulties.—Stalin.
                The Five-Year Plan of the food industry of the USSR.
Center: We will raise work productivity. We will realize the
                plan of great works.
Gauges: Salary + 69%; Cost of manufacturing - 33%;
                Productivity of labor + 110%

70
Elena Semenova
1929
Gosizdat [State Publishing House]
72.7 x 108.3 cm. (28 5/8 x 42 5/8 in.)

Top: In his workplace, every worker must vigilantly watch
                that his labor produces a cost reduction in
                manufactured articles.
Center: Some work badly, others better, the third [group] well.
Bottom: Catch up with the best and achieve a general increase.
                —Stalin.

71
Anonymous
c.1929
Moscow Regional Executive Commission
Edition: 15,000
71 x 105.6 cm. (27 15/16 x 41 9/16 in.)

Report of the Moscow Regional Executive Commission and the
Moscow Soviet.
Fulfill the Five-Year Plan in four years.
Graph Divisions:

	Top left:	Industry.
	Top right:	Agriculture.
	Center left:	Labor.
	Center right:	Budget.

РАБОТНИЦЫ—УДАРНИЦЫ,
КРЕПИТЕ УДАРНЫЕ БРИГАДЫ,
ОВЛАДЕВАЙТЕ ТЕХНИКОЙ,
УВЕЛИЧИВАЙТЕ КАДРЫ ПРОЛЕТАРСКИХ СПЕЦИАЛИСТОВ

72
Valentina Kulagina
1931
Ogiz-Izogiz [Combined State Publishing Houses]
Edition: 30,000
100 x 71.9 cm. (39 3/8 x 28 5/16 in.)

Women workers, women shock-workers [*udarnitsy*], strengthen the shock-brigades, master technology, increase the ranks of proletarian specialists.

73
Elizaveta and/or Boris Ignatovich
1931
Ogiz-Izogiz [Combined State Publishing Houses]
Edition: 20,000
51.3 x 71.7 cm. (20 1/4 x 28 1/4 in.)

Bottom: The struggle for the polytechnical school is the struggle for the Five-Year Plan, for the cadres, for class-based communist education.

Top right: Education linked with productive work is a powerful tool in the hands of the proletariat for the creation of the new person.

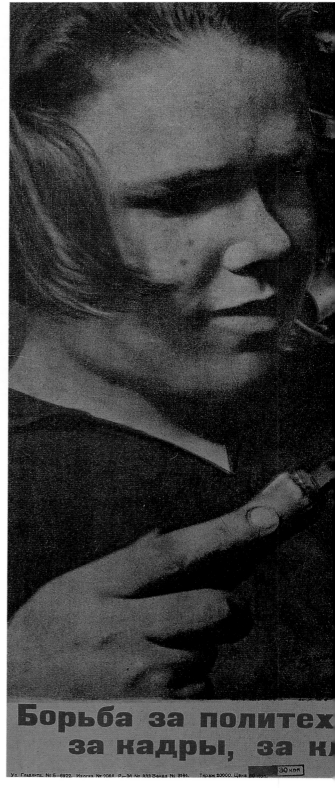

Борьба за политех
за кадры, за кл

СВЯЗЬ ОБУЧЕ-
НИЯ С ПРОИЗ-
ВОДИТЕЛЬ-
НЫМ ТРУ-
ДОМ — МОГУ-
ЧЕЕ ОРУДИЕ
В РУКАХ ПРО-
ЛЕТАРИАТА
ДЛЯ СОЗДА-
НИЯ НОВОГО
ЧЕЛОВЕКА

...ую школу есть борьба за пятилетку,
...ое коммунистическое воспитание

Огиз—Изогиз
Москва 1931 Ленинград

3-типо-литография ОГИЗа „Красный пролетарий" Москва.

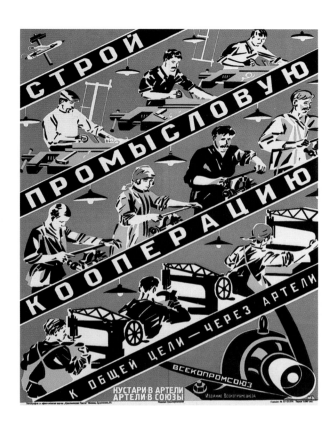

74
E. Lavinskaia, Elena Semenova
c.1928
Priboi [Surf], Leningrad
Edition: 20,000
106.7 x 71.1cm. (42 x 28 in.)

Top:	We will guard the electric conductor! The central electrical station is guarded, but the conductor is unprotected.
Lower left:	Any attack is enough to cause major damage to the economy of the whole region.
Lower right:	The factory is not working.There are fewer goods. Prices are raised. Damage to the conductor directly strikes the peasant's pocket.
Bottom:	Malicious saboteurs of the economic revival of workers and peasants cannot be spared.

75
Mechislav Dobrokovskii
Vsekopromsoiuz [All-Russian Cooperative Industrial Union]
Edition: 5,000
72.1 x 54.0 cm. (28 3/8 x 21 3/16 in.)

Build industrial cooperation. Towards the common goal through the cooperative associations [*arteli*]. Handicraftsmen [*kustari*] into cooperative associations. Cooperative associations into unions [*soiuzy*].

76
Valentina Kulagina
Gouache collage with photographic elements
18.1 x 28 cm. (7 1/8 x 11 in.)

Electro-combine.
Graph at left: Growth of the society of
                 inventors.

(Design for factory wall.)

77
B. Popov, I. Vilkovir
1931
Gouache collage with photographic elements
23.5 x 85.2 cm. (9 1/4 x 33 9/16 in.)

1. How the red stamp operator fullfills the
[six conditions] of the instructions of Stalin.
2. The best shock-workers [*udarnik*i]
3. False shock-workers [*udarniki*]
4. P.F.P. 1931
5. Inventors
6. Books for the shock-worker [*udarnik*]

(Design for factory wall.)

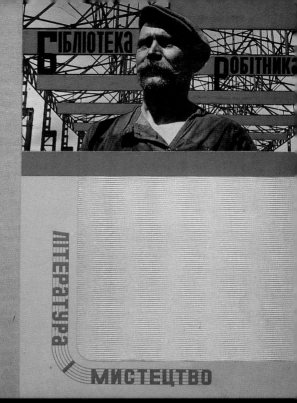
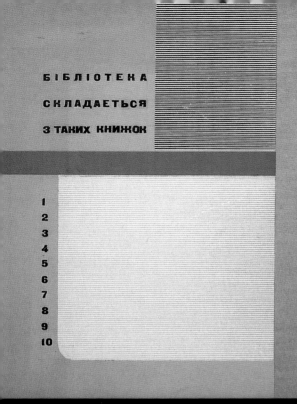

above:
78
Ermilov
Photomontage maquette
Mistetsvo
27 x 41.1 cm (10 5/8 x 16 1/16 in.)

Library of the worker. The library includes the following books:
[1–10].

(In Ukrainian.)

at left:
79
Lev Il'in
1929
46.2 x 31.8 cm. (18 3/16 x 12 1/2 in.)

Certificate of Commendation.
...The jury has found the participant [blank] in this exhibition
worthy of certification of commendation of the [blank] degree
for both the reflection of contemporaneity in the work and for
technical achievement.

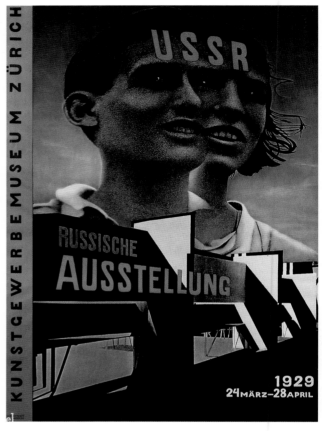

80
Anonymous
1928
Publishing House of the Central Committee of Metal-Workers
Edition: 10,000
61.9 x 47 cm. (243/8 x 181/2 in.)

Top: All metal-workers read their journal *Metal-Worker.*
Center: Subscriptions are open for:
Left: The daily journal *Metal-Worker.*
Right: The bi-weekly journal *Technology and the Metal-Worker.*
Right center:Subscription terms [for] *Metal-Worker* and *Technology and the Metal-Worker.*

above right:
81
El Lissitzky
1929
126.5 x 90.5 cm. (4913/16 x 355/8 in.)

Russian Exhibition. March 24–April 28, 1929. Applied Art Museum, Zurich.

(In German.)

at right:
82a, b
Anonymous
1933
Narkompros [The People's Commissariat of Enlightenment]
34.5 x 50.9 cm. (135/8 x 20)

(front and back cover)
To the *udarnik*—the cultural-soldier of the Second Five-Year Plan.
Bottom left: Through the methods of socialist competition [*sotssorevnovaniia*] and shock work [*udarnichestvo*], we will improve the quality of education to the highest degree, master the instrument of Marxist-Leninist theory, and use it to arm the working masses.

(inside spread)
"In a country of illiterate people, it is impossible to build a Communist socety."—Lenin
Top: The literacy department of the public education division awards student II class, Kulikova, Tamara, the honored title of shock-worker of the cultural revolution for excellent mastery of the curriculum and educational discipline....

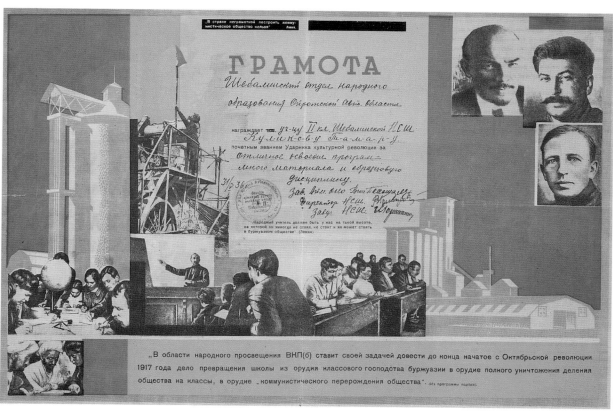

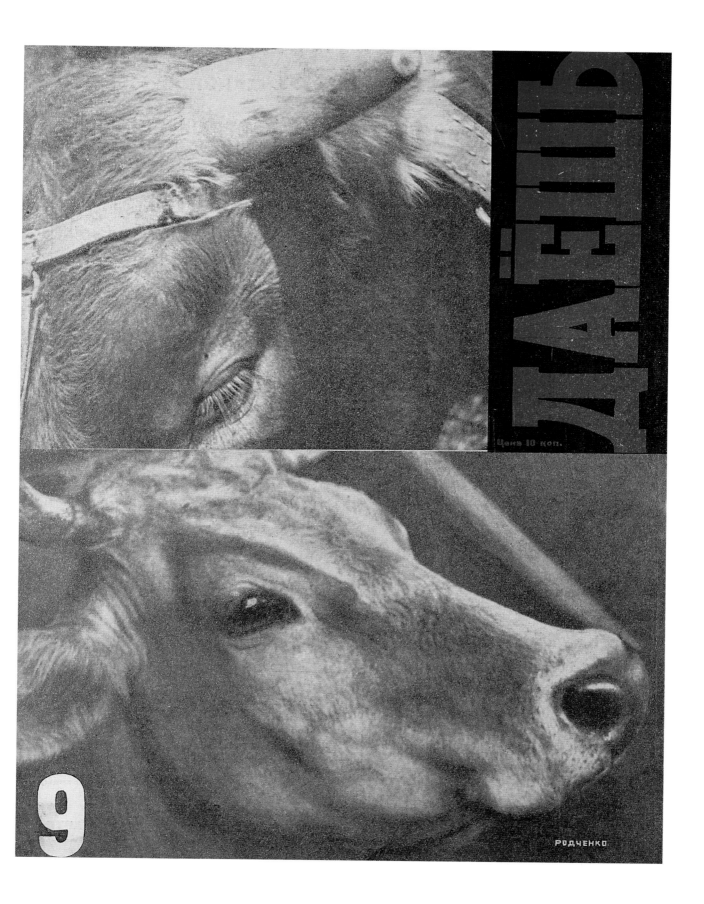

ДАЁШЬ 14

10 коп.

советский автомобиль

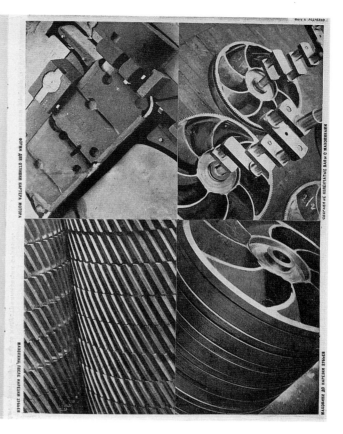

preceding pages, at left, and above:
83a–d
Aleksandr Rodchenko, Mechislav Dobrokovskii
1929
covers approx. 30.5 x 22.9 cm.
(approx.12 x 9 in.)
spread approx. 30.5 x 45.8 cm.
(approx. 12 x 18 in.)

Daesh' [Forward].

No. 6: Full Speed. Cover by Rodchenko.
No. 9: Cover by Rodchenko.
No. 14: Soviet Automobile. Cover by M. Dobrokovskii and
A. Rodchenko.
Inside spread by Rodchenko on the AMO [Moscow Automobile
Company] factory.

84
Nikolai Dolgorukov
1931
Ogiz-Izogiz [Combined State Publishing Houses]
Edition: 20,000
104.4 x 72.8 cm. (41 1/8 x 28 11/16 in.)

Transport worker, armed with technical knowledge, fight for the reconstruction of transport.

Top left: [Fulfill] the Five-Year Plan in four years.
Top right: There isn't a power in the world that the Bolsheviks couldn't beat.

85
Nikolai Dolgorukov
1931
Ogiz-Izogiz [Combined State Publishing Houses]
Edition: 15,000
105 x 74 cm. (41 3/8 x 29 3/16 in.)

Top: In 1932, the Ural-Kuznetskii Combine will give the country:
            4.5 million tons of pig-iron.
            2.5 million tons of coal.
            2.8 billion kilowatt-hours yield of electroenergy.
            10 thousand kilometers of railroad track.
Bottom: Let's create a powerful industrial base in the East!

at right:
86
Valentina Kulagina
1929
30.8 x 20.3 cm. (12 1/8 x 8 in.)

Red Field [*Krasnaia Niva*]-45. We are building.

87
Aleksandr Deineka
1930
Izogiz [State Publishing House for Art]
Edition: 50,000
109 x 77.3 cm. (42 15/16 x 30 1/2 in.)

Large text:	We will build the powerful Soviet dirigible "Klim Voroshilov."
Small text:	The dirigible is a powerful weapon for defense and cultural construction. We need to catch up to and surpass capitalist countries in the area of dirigible-building. Every worker must take active part in the realization of this great deed...

(General Kliment Voroshilov was the head of the Soviet Armed Forces.)

88
Leonid Chupiatov
1931
Izogiz [State Publishing House for Art]
Edition: 15,000
70 x 103 cm. (27 7/8 x 40 1/2 in.)

Top:	Set a Bolshevik pace in preparation for the sowing.
Bottom:	For the organization of new M.T.S. [Machine Tractor Stations]—Strong points of complete collectivization and, on this basis, of the liquidation of kulaks as a class.

(Collectivization was the Soviet agricultural policy of the late 1920s and early 1930s. It entailed the forced transformation of individual peasant farms into large state owned socialist farms through the formation of cooperatives. Hand in hand with collectivization was the policy of "dekulakization," i.e. the liquation of the kulaks [peasants labelled as wealthy] as an alien class hostile to the poor peasants and the Bolsheviks. Liquidation meant eviction followed by one of several options: imprisonment in labor camps, execution, or deportation and resettlement in remote areas.)

89
Brigade KGK-3
1931
Ogiz-Izogiz
[Combined State Publishing Houses]
Edition: 60,000
70 x 100 cm. (27 5/8 x 39 3/4 in.)

Top: Free working hands of the
             collective farms, to industry!
Bottom left: Contract...
Bottom right: From a haphazard "policy,"
             we must proceed to a policy
             of organized recruitment of
             workers for industry. But only
             one path exists for this—the
             path of contracts between
             economic organizations and
             collective farms, and experi-
             ence shows that in practice,
             contracts provide significant
             results both for collective
             farms and for industrial
             enterprises.
             —From Stalin's speech at the
             economic conference of
             June 23, 1931.

90
Gustav Klutsis
1930/31
Izogiz [State Publishing House for Art]
105.4 x 74.8 cm. (41 1/2 x 21 7/16 in.)

Young Communists [*Komsomol'tsi*], to an accelerated sowing!

(In Ukrainian.)

*(*Komsomol'tsi *were members of the Communist League of Youth—the Komsomol.)*

at right:
91
Gustav Klutsis
1930
Izogiz [State Publishing House for Art]
Edition: 20,000
101.6 x 71.3 cm. (40 x 28 1/8 in.)

We will repay the coal debt to the country.

92
Gustav Klutsis
1931
Photomontage maquette
25.4 x 35.6 cm. (10 x 14 in.)

The reality of our program is active people—
is you and us [together].

(In pencil.)

93a
Gustav Klutsis
1931
Photomontage maquette
24.1 x 16.5 cm. (9 1/2 x 6 1/2 in.)

See no. 93b

at right:
93b
Gustav Klutsis
1931
Izogiz [State Publishing House for Art]
Edition: 20,000
142.4 x 103.5 cm. (56 1/16 x 40 3/4 in.)

Top: The reality of our program is
active people—is you and us
[together].

Below: Six conditions for victory:
1) The organized assembling of
the work force.
2) The destruction of
egalitarianism.
3) The liquidation of the lack of
personal responsibility.
4) The creation of our own
manufacturing intelligentsia.
5) The bestowing of greater
attention to older specialists.
6) The strengthening of the
self-supporting economy.

94
A. Rostovtsov
Leningrad Gublit [Regional Department for
Literary and Publishing Affairs]
Edition: 2,000
37.5 x 45.7 cm. (14 3/4 x 18 in.)

Let's revive aeronautics. Our first [air]ship,
the Vladimir Il'ich.

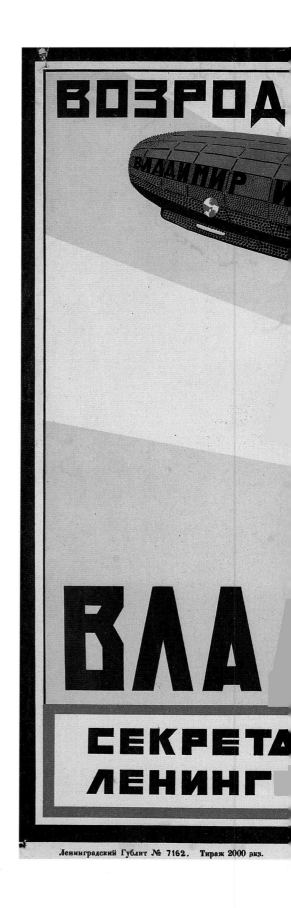

ВОЗДУХОПЛАВАНИЕ

НАШ ПЕРВЫЙ КОРАБЛЬ

СССР

МИР ИЛЬИЧ

О.Д.В.Ф. — С.З.О.
СМОЛЬНЫЙ К.7

ТЕЛ.183-28
ПРИЕМ
ОТ 10-4 Ч.

А.РОСТОВЦОВ.

Типо-Литография Акад. Худ. (арендов. у Промбюро), Тучков пер. д. № 1.

Работать, строить
и не ныть!
Нам к новой жизни
путь указан.
Атлетом можешь
ты не быть,
Но физкультурником —
обязан.

at right:
96
Gitsevich
1932
Ogiz-Izogiz [Combined State Publishing Houses]
Edition: 15,000
102.5 x 70.2 cm. (40 3/8 x 27 11/16 in.)

Left: For the socialist forge of health.
Bottom: For the proletarian park of
            culture and leisure.
Armband: "Mass Organizer."

at left:
95
Aleksandr Deineka
1933
Ogiz-Izogiz [Combined State Publishing Houses]
98.4 x72.4 cm. (38 3/4 x 28 1/2 in.)

Work, build, and don't whine. The path to
a new life is shown to us. You might not
become an athlete, but you are obliged to
become a sportsman [*fizkul'turnik*].

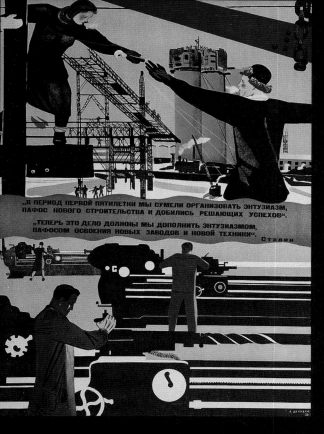

98
Aleksandr Deineka
1933
Ogiz-Izogiz [Combined State Publishing Houses]
Edition: 23,000
103.8 x 73.2 cm. (407/8 x 2813/16 in.)

"During the period of the Five-Year Plan we were able to organize
enthusiasm and zeal [*pafos*] for new construction and achieved
decisive success. Now we must add to this with enthusiasm and
zeal in the mastery of new factories and new technology."—Stalin

at left:
97
Anonymous [Aleksandr Alekseev?]
1930
Edition: 30, 000
104.5 x 71.8 cm. (411/8 x 281/4 in.)

Bottom: By actively participating in the unfolding socialist offensive
           through the factory-kitchen and laundry, cinema and
           radio, and supporting the factory and collective farm, the
           consumers' cooperative suitably commemorates the XIII
           anniversary of October.
Large letters: Cooperation.
On buildings: Collective farm, bread-factory, elevator, laundry,

99
Dmitrii Moor
1934
Ogiz-Izogiz [Combined State Publishing Houses]
Edition: 40,000
87.6 x 60 cm. (341/2 x 235/8 in.)

We were a country of the plough, we have become a country of the
tractor and combine. (Kaganovich)

*(One of Stalin's staunchest supporters, Lazar Kaganovich was
Moscow Party chief and a member of the Politburo from 1930 to
1935.)*

100
Mariia Bri-Bein
1931
Ogiz-Izogiz [Combined State Publishing Houses]
Edition: 30,000
86.4 x 59.5 cm. (34 x 237/16 in.)

Woman worker, woman collective-farm worker, behind the wheel of
the tractor, at the work bench, with the rifle, be a shock-worker
[*udarnitsa*] of defense.

101
Aleksei Kokorekin
1932
Ogiz-Izogiz [Combined State Publishing Houses]
Edition: 40,000
109 x 77 cm. (43 x 305/8 in.)

Center: Fighters and commanders of the Red Army, bring to
            life the slogan of comrade Stalin: "Bolsheviks must
            master technology."
Bottom: Technology in the hands of the Red Army strengthens
            its might and guarantees the inviolability of Soviet
            borders.

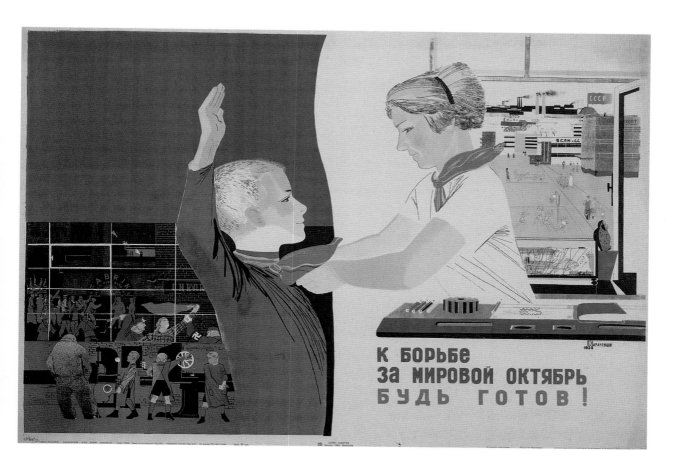

102
Karachentsov
1933
Ogiz-Izogiz [Combined State Publishing Houses]
Edition: 50,000
76.4 x 109.4 cm. (30 1/8 x 43 1/8 in.)

Be prepared for the battle for world-wide October!

103
Gustav Klutsis
Photomontage
10.2 x 33.4 cm. (4 x 13 1/8 in.)

Higher, banners of Marx, Engels, Lenin, and Stalin.
Beneath Marx: Vive la Commune!
Beneath Engels: Vive la Commune!
Beneath Lenin: All power to the Soviets.
Beneath Stalin: To battle for the Second Five-Year Plan.

104
M. Razulevich
1932
Ogiz [Association of State Publishing Houses]-"Young Guard"
21 x 38.7 cm. (8 1/4 x 15 1/4 in.)

"The reality of our program is active people—is you and us
[together], our will to work, our readiness to work in a new way,
our resolution to fulfill the Plan."—Stalin

at left:
105a
M. Razulevich
1933
Photomontage maquette
22.9 x 49.7 cm. (9 x 19 9/16 in.)

10 Years Without Lenin.

105b
M. Razulevich
1933
Lenpartizdat [Leningrad Party Press]
22.3 x 49.3 cm. (8 13/16 x 19 7/16 in.)

Z. Pindrik and S. Tiul'panov. *10 Years Without Lenin.*

above left:
106
Viktor Deni, Nikolai Dolgorukov
1935
Ogiz-Izogiz [Combined State Publishing Houses]
Edition: 10,000
99.1 x 69.7 cm. (39 x 27 1/2 in.)

Left: Long live our great Stalin!
Right: There is no fortress which the Bolsheviks could not take.—Stalin
Center: The Metro is here!

(The Metro, opened in 1935, was part of a general project for the "reconstruction" of Moscow in early 1930s, headed largely by Lazar Kaganovich—the figure who appears to the left of Stalin in this poster. At this time, the Ministry of Transportation was under his authority.)

above right:
107
Gustav Klutsis
1932
Ogiz-Izogiz [Combined State Publishing Houses]
Edition: 15,000
150 x 108.5 cm. (59 1/16 x 42 3/4 in.)

Greeting to those who have joined the work at the world-wide giant Dneprostroi DGES [the construction site of the Dneiper Hydro-Electric Station].
Long live the shock-workers [*udarniki*] of socialist construction.

108
Boris Belopol'skii
1933/34
"Art" Publishing House, Kharkov
Edition: 10,000
72 x 106 cm. (28 3/8 x 42 in.)

Strive for still greater sucess in the business
of nurturing the female proletarian mass in
the spirit of struggle for the full majesty of
socialism. In the spirit of carrying out the
behest of our teacher Lenin. (Stalin)

ЦЕ БОЛЬШИХ „УСПЕХОВ В ДЕЛЕ ВОСПИТАНИЯ ЖЕНСКИХ
ИХ МАСС В ДУХЕ БОРЬБЫ ЗА ПОЛНОЕ ТОРЖЕСТВО
А, В ДУХЕ ВЫПОЛНЕНИЯ ВЕЛИКИХ ЗАВЕТОВ НАШЕГО
ИНА.   (СТАЛИН).

Цена 1 руб. 20 коп.   Сдано в печать 14/XII—33 г. Подписано в печать 23/г —34 г. Ф. 72×110—1 — 66 к/л.   Главлит № 7481 (1316)   Киев. 5-я тип УПП ДВОУ — Зак. № 3006. Тир. 10000

109
Natal'ia Pinus
1933
Ogiz-Izogiz [Combined State Publishing
Houses]
Edition: 40,000
80.5 x 162 cm. (31 3/4 x 63 13/16 in.)

Top: Women in the collective
farms are a great force
(J. Stalin)

Bottom: Women in collective farms
are a great force. To restrain
this force is to permit a
crime. Our responsibility is to
advance women in collective
farms and to put this force in
motion.—J. Stalin

ABOUT THE COLLECTION

Merrill C. Berman's collection of graphic art rivals that of major museums in breadth, quality, and scholarly focus. It is distinguished, however, from such institutional collections in the openness of its embrace of explicitly political images. Throughout Berman's holdings, works provide evidence of a tenacious interest in the relationship between art and the social world (an interest that one might say is left-leaning, as Berman's collection is particularly strong in not only Soviet graphic design, but German Communist design from the thirties, and American WPA design.) This undoubtedly derives in part from Berman's own maturation as a collector.

Born into a family of avid antiquers, Berman began to collect American political ephemera as a teenager, building the foundation for a collection that is now considered one of the most important of its kind. He pursued this interest until entering college, then laid it aside. If the collecting impulse came from his family as a whole, Berman's interest in politics was fostered in particular by his father, who was active in Democratic state politics (a friend and supporter of Henry Wallace, who ran against Harry Truman for President) and an early member of the NAACP. At Harvard College, Berman's enthusiasm for all things political was honed by studying with such prominent figures as Merle Fainsod, George Kennan, Paul Tillich, Louis Hartz, Karl Friedrich, and McGeorge Bundy.

Art history was notably absent form Berman's formal education; far from limiting his vision, this probably freed it from aesthetic preconceptions which may have led to a rejection of overtly political design. Berman regards his early experience with political ephemera as his main education in graphic design, sharpening his eye for typography and the use of color and implanting an interest in the ways designers attempted to communicate to a mass audience.

After graduation, Berman turned momentarily to the collection of paintings. But when a stock-market crash forced him to sell these works, he returned to his first collecting interest—political ephemera—and soon broadened his scope to include graphic art in general. It was partly a financial decision; building a collection of paintings by well-known artists required staggering resources, whereas a modest sum could go far in graphic design. But, for Berman, this was also a move to a relatively open and undocumented field, where he could make a personal contribution by researching and tracking down material from all over the world to create a collection that would raise public awareness of the varieties of practice in the graphic arts. Berman became an active and scholarly collector with a sense of personal mission, and today his collection ranges from American nineteenth-century broadsides to contemporary Japanese design, with Viennese Secession exhibition graphics, spare de Stijl and Bauhaus work, and Polish posters of the 1960s and 70s in between.

Soon after his return to collecting graphic art, Berman came across a trove of Russian posters that included seminal works by Gustav Klutsis, Aleksandr Deineka, and others. "Distinctly non-decorative and...trying to communicate something," as Berman says, they struck him immediately as important to the history of modern poster design. Trying to find out more information about these Russian works, he visited the Museum of Modern Art, where the then-curator of graphic design urged him to concentrate on less political work, film posters perhaps. Characteristically, this rebuff strengthened Berman's conviction to give these works the credit they were due. At the time, the 1970s, Berman was one of the few collectors in the field. As multiples made for mass consumption, graphic design in itself was considered a poor cousin within the art market. And a lingering Cold War belief in the "evil empire" made posters from the Soviet Union, especially explicitly political ones, less than desirable. "During the heavy Brezhnev years," says Berman, "artists like Klutsis and Deineka were almost taboo." But in recent years, the dissolution of the Soviet Union has both opened markets and tempered latent ideological resistance. "With the breakdown, things have begun to seem more benign, even romantic—like the Berlin Wall."

The market for Soviet graphic design has evolved with a similar, dizzying rapidity. Already by the 1970s, a handful of émigrés had set up shop as dealers in the West; and now because of post-Soviet economic chaos, the market is wide open. Prices have risen markedly as a variety of collectors and dealers have entered the field. There is also a growing interest in Soviet graphic design from scholars and curators. Berman credits this to recent historical events, but it is also his collection which has laid much of the groundwork to make serious consideration of Soviet design possible.

I am profoundly grateful to Merrill Berman for his willing and enthusiastic support of this exhibition, and for his encouragement in general.

Leah Dickerman

ARTIST BIOGRAPHIES

NATAN ISAEVICH AL'TMAN (1889–1970)

Al'tman began his artistic training at the Odessa School of Art where he studied from 1901 to 1907. He exhibited with the First Izdebskii International Salon in 1909–10 and with the Society of Southern Russian Artists in 1910. Along with Vladimir Tatlin and Lev Bruni, he was a member of the group Apartment No. 5. He traveled to Paris in 1910, where he attended the Free Russian Academy of Marie Wassilieff until 1912 and exhibited at the salon of the Société National des Beaux-Arts in 1911. Upon returning to Russia, he participated in the World of Art exhibitions of 1913 and 1915, and at several avant-garde shows, including the Union of Youth in 1913–14, the Tramway V and 0.10 exhibitions in 1915, and the Knave of Diamonds group shows in 1916 and 1917. Along with the artists Sergei Isakov, Nikolai Punin, the poet-designer Vladimir Maiakovskii, the director Vsevolod Meyerhold, and the composer Sergei Prokofiev, he founded the Freedom of Art Association in Petrograd. From 1918 to 1920 he taught at the Petrograd SVOMAS [the State Free Art Workshops]. In 1918 he created public decorations for the first anniversary of the Revolution. He was also active in IZO Narkompros [the Department of Fine Art of the Commissariat of Enlightenment] and its journal *Iskusstvo kommuny* [Art of the Commune (1918–19)]. In January he joined the *Komfut* [Communist-Futurist] group, which included the theorists Osip Brik and Boris Kushner, Maiakovskii, and the painter David Shterenberg.

Al'tman was in charge of the decoration of Petrograd to celebrate May Day 1919. A member of the Moscow INKhUK [Institute of Artistic Culture], he spoke about his theatrical decorations on May 11, 1922. Along with Shterenberg and Naum Gabo, he was commissioner for the First Exhibition of Russian Art in Berlin. He collaborated with Marc Chagall and Shterenberg in 1922 on the Group of Three exhibition. In 1925, he participated in the Exposition international des arts décoratifs et industriels modernes in Paris in 1925 (for which he won a gold medal), and the seventh exhibition of the group L'Araignée [The Spider] at the Galerie Devambe in Paris the same year. A monographical exhibition of his work was organized in Leningrad in 1926. From 1928 to 1935 he worked in Paris. He exhibited at the jubilee exhibition Artists of the RSFSR Over Fifteen Years, held at the Russian Museum, Leningrad in 1932. In 1936 he returned to Leningrad and designed the sets for theatrical productions, and illustrated and designed books. He was awarded a gold medal at the 1937 International Exposition in Paris.

BORIS BELOPOL'SKII (1909–?)

Belopol'skii studied painting and graphic work at the art school in Kharkov until 1928, after which he was active as an artist and designer in Moscow.

MARIIA FELIKSOVNA BRI-BEIN (1892–?)

Bri-Bein studied art in Odessa and Moscow. From 1926 she was a member of the AKhRR [the Association of Artists of Revolutionary Russia], an organization that advocated a new heroic realism based on nineteenth-century models of painting. From 1930 on, she designed posters, and in 1934, won first prize in a poster competition commemorating the tenth anniversary of Lenin's death.

LEONID TERENTEVICH CHUPIATOV (1890–1941)

Chupiatov studied at the school of the Society for the Encouragement of the Arts in St. Petersburg from 1909 to 1912. In 1916 he studied at the Bershtein school where Natan Al'tman taught. Following the Revolution, between 1918 and 1921, he worked under Kuzma Petrov-Vodkin at the Petrograd SVOMAS [the State Free Art Workshops]. He participated in the First State Free Exhibition of Artworks in Petrograd in 1919. From 1918 to 1920 he taught at the Art School of the Baltic Fleet. His work was included in the enormous survey, Exhibition of Paintings by Petrograd Artists of All Tendencies, 1919–1923, held in Petrograd in 1923. Between 1926 and 1928 he taught at the Kiev Art Institute. He was represented in the major exhibition in Moscow in 1927 commemorating the tenth anniversary of the Revolution. In 1929 he taught at the Academy of Art and was included in the jubilee exhibition Artists of the RSFSR Over Fifteen Years, held at the Russian Museum, Leningrad in 1932. He taught at GINKhUK [State Institute of Artistic Culture] after 1933.

ALEKSANDR ALEKSANDROVICH DEINEKA (1899–1969)

Born in Kursk, Deineka studied at Kharkov Art School from 1915 until 1917, and at the VKhUTEMAS [Higher Sate Artistic and Technical Workshops in Moscow] from 1921 until 1925. He made easel paintings and drawings, sculptural pieces, mosaics, frescoes, and stained-glass displays, and was prolific as a book illustrator. He served in the Red Army at the defense of Kursk against the Whites in 1919–20. He moved to Moscow, where he was a founding member of OST (the Society of Easel Painters, 1925–28), a founding member of the *Oktiabr'* [October] group from 1928 to 1930, and a member of RAPKh [the Russian Association of Proletarian Artists] from 1931 until 1932. Deineka exhibited with the Group of Three (Deineka, Yuri Pimenov, and Andrei Goncharov) at the First Discussional Exhibition of Associations of Active Revolutionary Art in 1924, and at the seventh exhibition of the group *L'Araignée* [The Spider] at the Galerie Devambe in Paris in 1925. He also displayed work at the International Exhibition in Dresden in 1926 and took part in the major exhibition in Moscow commemorating the tenth anniversary of the Revolution. In the twenties and thirties he contributed to the magazines *Bezbozhnik u Stanka* [Atheist at the Bench], *Smena* [Young Generation], and *Daesh'* [Forward]. He lived in Moscow after 1920, and traveled to France and Italy between 1925 and 1936, to the USA in 1935, and to Germany, Austria, and Italy after World War II. Deineka painted panels for the Soviet Pavilion at the 1937 Paris International Exhibition and for an exhibition in Minsk in 1938. In Moscow, he taught at VKhUTEIN [Higher State Artistic and Technical Institute (1928–30)], at the Polygraphic Institute (1928–34), at the Institute of Fine Art (1934–46; 1957–63), at the Institute of Applied and Decorative Art (1945–53), and at the Architectural Institute (1953–57). Deineka was the recipient of numerous honors, including being named People's Artist of the USSR in 1963, a Hero of Socialist Labor in 1963, and he received a Lenin Prize in 1964.

VIKTOR NIKOLAEVICH DENI (1893–1946)

Deni, whose last name was originally Denisov, was born to an impoverished gentry family. At school, he developed an interest in naturalist painters like Il'ia Repin and Valentin Serov and studied under visiting teachers. In 1906 he began to exhibit with the Association of Independent Artists, and in 1910, contributed satirical illustrations to journals. After moving to Moscow, he was involved in designing for the theater, began to publish regularly in journals, and was named artistic director of the satirical weekly, *Bich* [Sword]. Under the direction of an anti-Bolshevik general editor, *Bich* was closed in the wake of the October Revolution. Deni approached Anatoli Lunacharskii, the People's Commissar of Enlightenment, to offer his services to the new regime, and was given work under Revvoensovet [the Revolutionary-Military Council of the Republic] in the Volga military district. Deni created nearly fifty posters for the Red cause during the Civil War between 1918 and 1921. After 1920 he became more involved with newspaper cartoons and from 1921, contributed regularly to the *Pravda* [Truth], *Izvestiia* [News], *Krasnaia niva* [Red Field], and *Krokodil* [Crocodile] periodicals. Deni was named an Honored Art Worker of the Russian Federation in 1932.

MECHISLAV VASIL'EVICH DOBROKOVSKII (1895–1937)

Dobrovkovskii's work was included in the Exposition international des arts décoratifs et industriels modernes in Paris in 1925 and at the seventh anniversary of the group *L'Araignée* [The Spider] at the Galerie Devambe in Paris that same year. He was a member of the Society of Easel Painters [OST], a group that insisted on the continued importance of painting in post-Revolutionary Russia, but advocated a new, modern style. He was listed as a member of the *Oktiabr'* [October] group, and frequently contributed drawings and cover designs to the journal *Daesh'* [Forward] during its run in 1929.

NIKOLAI ANDREEVICH DOLGORUKOV (1902–1980)

Dolgorukov studied at VKhUTEIN [Higher State Artistic and Technical Institute in Moscow] from 1928 to 1932. He was active as a poster designer from the early thirties and contributed illustrations and satirical drawings to *Pravda* [Truth] and other periodicals. In the mid-thirties he collaborated with Viktor Deni on a series of posters. In 1963 he was named an Honored Art Worker of the Russian Federation.

GUSTAV GUSTAVOVICH KLUTSIS (1895–1938)

Born near Riga in Latvia, Klutsis began his artistic training at the Art School of Riga in 1912 and attended the school administered by the Society for the Encouragement of the Arts in Petrograd from 1915 to 1917. A participant in both the February and October Revolutions, Klutsis enlisted in 1917 in the Ninth Regiment of Latvian Rifles and took part in the defense of Smol'nyi, against anti-Bolshevik forces. A year later he was summoned to Moscow to help defend the Kremlin during the Civil War. For May Day 1918, Klutsis sketched Lenin and his fellow soldiers and designed posters and decorations. He participated in the art studio of Vol'demar Andersen and displayed his work at the Regiment's first exhibition. In August 1918 he entered the second SVO-MAS [State Free Art Workshops] in Moscow, studying first with Kostatin Korovin, then with Kazimir Malevich, and lastly with Antoine Pevsner, who took over the studio after Malevich left for Vitebsk in the Summer of 1919. There he met the artist Valentina Kulagina, whom he later married. Klutsis's first photomontage, "The Dynamic City," dates from this time. Along with Pevsner and Naum Gabo, Klutsis exhibited his work in 1920 on Tverskoi Boulevard in Moscow. Visiting Malevich in Vitebsk, he showed his work with Malevich's Suprematist UNOVIS group [Affirmers of the New Art] in Vitebsk in 1920 and in Moscow in 1921. In 1921 he joined the Communist Party and a year later graduated from the VKhUTEMAS. Klutsis opened a studio with Sergei Sen'kin within VKhUTEMAS, which advocated concepts developed by UNOVIS. In 1922 Klutsis designed a series of agitational stands to celebrate the fifth anniversary of the Revolution and the Fourth Congress of the Comintern. Also during that year he exhibited at the First Russian Art Exhibition in Berlin. In 1923, Klutsis and Sen'kin established the *Masterskaia revoliutsii* [Workshop of the Revolution] within the VKhUTEMAS to train artists to fulfill contemporary political needs. He taught color theory in the Wood and Metalworking Faculty of VKhUTEMAS from 1924 to 1930. In 1925 Klutsis helped organize the Russian contribution to the Exposition international des arts décoratifs et industriels modernes in Paris. He was also associated with the Constructivist journal *Lef* [Left (1923–25)]. During the 1920s, Klutsis became increasingly involved in the theory and practice of photomontage, using it extensively in his posters and decorations for revolutionary festivals. Klutsis participated in the Pressa exhibition in Cologne (1928), in Film und Foto in Stuttgart (1929), and in Photomontage in Berlin (1931). In 1928 he was a founder of the *Oktiabr'* [October] group, and showed work in its 1930 exhibition. From 1929 to 1932 he was vice-president of the Association of Revolutionary Poster Artists. Klutsis was arrested in 1938 and executed soon afterwards.

ALEKSEI ALEKSEEVICH KOKOREKIN (1906–1959)

Kokorekin graduated from the Kuban Secondary School of Art Teachers in 1929 and began designing political posters in 1930. In addition, he produced books, architectural decorations, and paintings. He was named Honored Art Worker of the Russian Federation in 1956 and was a USSR State Prize Winner.

VLADIMIR IVANOVICH KOZLINSKII (1891–1967)

Kozlinskii studied at the Society for the Encouragement of the Arts, the Zvanteseva School, and privately under D.N. Kardovskii. He showed works in the Triangle exhibition in St. Petersburg in 1909 and impressionist exhibition organized by Nikolai Kul'bin in Vilno in 1909–10. By 1911 he was studying under the printmaker Vasilii Mate in St. Petersburg. After the Revolution, Kozlinskii worked on decorations for revolutionary festivals and became the head of the engraving studio at SVOMAS [the State Free Art Workshops]. In 1918, he collaborated with Vladimir Maiakovskii on the satirical taxonomy, *Heroes and Victims of the Revolution*. The same year he showed works at an exhibition of Russian landscape painting in Petrograd and in 1919 at the First State Free Exhibition of Artworks, also in Petrograd. In 1920, Kozlinskii joined the ROSTA collaborative in Petrogad, and along with Vladimir Lebedev and Lev Brodaty directed the activities of the agency in that city. Two years later, Kozlinskii exhibited with the Union of New Tendencies in Art in Petrograd and was represented at the First Russian Exhibition in Berlin. In 1925 he participated in the Third Exhibition of Paintings by Artists from Kaluga and Moscow and in the Seventh Exhibition of *L'Araignee* [The Spider] at the Galerie Devambe in Paris. In 1928, he was represented at the exhibit which marked the tenth Anniversary of the Revolution in Moscow.

VALENTINA NIKIFOROVNA KULAGINA (1902–1987)

Kulagina studied in the studios of Antoine Pevsner and Vladimir Favorski in the SVO-MAS [Higher State Artistic and Technical Workshops in Moscow] in 1919, then at the VKhUTEMAS during 1920 and 1921 with Gustav Klutsis, whom she later married. She exhibited her first photomontage works and constructivist typography in 1925. In 1928, Kulagina participated in the organization of the Soviet section of the Pressa exhibition in Cologne, Germany. She became a member of the *Oktiabr'* [October] group in 1928, showing in their exhibition in Moscow in 1930. From the late twenties, Kulagina produced political posters through Izogiz [the State Publishing House for Art], sometimes collaborating with Klutsis. In 1931, she participated in the Photomontage exhibition in Berlin, and in 1932, she was included in the Moscow exhibition, Posters in the Service of the Five-Year Plan. Until the end of the 1930s, she created posters and participated in numerous exhibitions in the USSR and elsewhere. After the arrest and internment of Klutsis, she disappeared from public life.

ALEKSEI LEVIN (1893–1965)

Levin was born in Sebastopol. He studied at the Odessa School of Art from 1904 to 1915 and at Moscow College from 1915 to 1918. He joined the Moscow ROSTA collaborative where he encountered Vladimir Maiakovskii, with whom he was later to collaborate on a number of literacy and advertising posters. Levin's work was represented in a typographic exhibition in Cologne, Germany in 1928.

EL LISSITZKY (LAZAR MARKOVICH LISITSKII) (1890–1941)

Lissitzky was born at Pochinok, near Smolensk, to a middle-class Jewish family. He studied art from 1903 with Yuri Pen, who also taught Marc Chagall. After being turned away by the St. Petersburg Academy in 1909, Lissitzky went to Germany and studied architecture at the Technische Hochschule in Darmstadt from 1909 to 1914. His first exhibition was in St. Petersburg with the Union of Artists in 1912. During the next two years he lived in Paris, where he met Osip Zadkine, and travelled to Italy. He returned to Russia in 1914 and worked briefly in Zadkine's studio in Vitebsk. Declared unfit for military service, he studied at the Riga Polytechnical Institute from about 1915 to 1917. In 1917 he exhibited in Moscow with *Mir iskusstva* [the World of Art group]. In the years immediately following the Revolution he was involved in many Jewish cultural activities, helping to establish the Yiddish publishing house Kultur Lige in 1919, the Society for the Encouragement of Jewish Art, and the Exhibition of Paintings and Sculpture by Jewish Artists. In 1918 he joined IZO Narkompros [the Department of Fine Art of the Commissariat of Enlightenment] and in May 1919 he went, at Chagall's invitation, to teach architecture and graphics at the Vitebsk Art School. After Kazimir Malevich's arrival in 1919, Lissitzky was attracted to Suprematism and became a member of Malevich's UNOVIS group [Affirmers of the New Art]. Inspired by Malevich and Suprematism, in 1919–20 Lissitzky developed his

PROUN [Project for the Affirmation of the New], which he declared "a half-way station between architecture and painting." While in Vitebsk he also designed decorations for the revolutionary festivals and agitational posters. Lissitzky joined the Moscow INKhUK [Institute of Artistic Culture], where he delivered a paper explaining his new concept of PROUN. In 1921 he began teaching at the Moscow VKhUTEMAS [Higher State Artistic and Technical Workshops]. In 1922, Lissitzky left Moscow for Berlin, where he founded the journal *Veshch'* [Object] with the writer Il'ia Erenberg. Lissitzky traveled extensively between Russia and Europe in the 1920s, establishing important contacts with the western avant-garde: with Dada artists at the Congress in Düsseldorf, with de Stijl artists in Holland, and with the Bauhaus in Weimar. In 1922 he participated in the First Russian Art Exhibit in Berlin, for which he designed the catalog cover. For the Great Berlin Art Exhibition in 1923, Lissitzky designed an entire PROUN room. He designed covers for *Broom* (1922), published articles on PROUNS in *De Stijl* magazine and collaborated with Mies van der Rohe on the magazine *G*. He designed the layout for Vladimir Maiakovskii's book of poetry, *Dlia golosa* [For the Voice], in 1923. In 1924, while recovering from tuberculosis, Lissitzky worked on Kurt Schwitters's magazine *Merz*, edited *Die Kunstismen* with Hans Arp, and worked with Mart Stam and others on the journal *ABC. Essays on Building*. In 1925 Lissitzky returned to Russia. From 1925 until 1930 he taught the design of architectural interiors and furniture design in the Wood and Metalwork faculty of the Moscow VKhUTEMAS. Around 1926 he edited with Nikolai Ladovskii the first and only issue of the journal *ASNOVA News* [Association of New Architects]. In the same year he traveled to Germany and installed a room of modern art at the International Art display at Dresden. From 1928 to 1930, he was engaged in projects for the interiors of communal housing blocks and his design for an interior of the flats in Mosei Ginzburg and Ignatii Milinis' House for the Employees of the Commissariat of France in Moscow. In 1929 he worked on a model for Vsevolod Meyerhold's proposed production of Sergei Tret'iakov's "I Want a Child." He became increasingly involved in exhibition design in the later 1920s: creating the "Abstract Room" for the Internationale Kunstaustellung (Dresden, 1926); organizing the Soviet display at the Pressa exhibition (Cologne, 1928); designing the Russian Typographical Exhibition (Moscow, 1927); the Soviet sections at Film und Foto (Stuttgart, 1929), the Internationale Hygiene-Austellung (Dresden, 1930), and the Internationale Pelz-Austellung (Leipzig, 1930). In 1928 he traveled to Europe and met Piet Mondrian and Le Corbusier. From the early 1930s Lissitzky experimented with collage, photography, photograms, and photomontage, organizing the typographical and photographic layouts for such magazines as *SSSR na stroike* [USSR in Construction], for which he worked from 1932 onwards. He joined the *Oktiabr'* [October] group in 1928, and in 1930 participated in an *Oktiabr'* group exhibition and also published a survey of Soviet architecture, *Russia: The Reconstruction of Architecture in the Soviet Union*. In 1931 he showed work in the Photomontage exhibition in Berlin. Lissitzky continued to work in the 1930s in graphic and exhibition design, even as his health was deteriorating. He was appointed artist-architect for the Gor'kii Park of Culture and Leisure in Moscow and for the Agricultural Exhibition of 1934.

VLADIMIR VLADIMIROVICH MAIAKOVSKII (1893–1930)

Maiakovskii joined the Bolshevik Party in 1908, at the age of fifteen. In 1911, he studied at the Moscow School of Painting, Sculpture, and Architecture, where he met David Burliuk and joined Burliuk's Cubo-Futurist group, Hylaea. Maiakovskii recited poetry with the group, and in 1912 he collaborated on the Futurist manifesto "A Slap in the Face of Public Taste." In the years before 1917, Maiakovskii wrote several books, magazine articles, works for the theater, and numerous poems. After the October Revolution, Maiakovskii was one of the first members of the avant-garde to agree to work with the Bolsheviks; he joined IZO Narkompros [the Department of Fine Art of the Commissariat of Enlightenment] and collaborated on a number of that agency's publishing ventures. In 1918, he wrote the play *Mystery-Bouffe*, an allegory about the Revolution, which was performed on the anniversary of the October Revolution. It was produced in 1918 in Petrograd by Vsevolod Meyerhold, with theatrical designs by Kazimir Malevich. From 1918 to 1922, Maiakovskii was a leading figure in the poster-making collaborative of ROSTA [the Russian Telegraph Agency]. In January 1919, he was a founding member of the *Komfut* [Communist-Futurist] group in Petrograd. In 1923, he was one of the founders of *Lef* [Left] magazine, which brought literary and political theorists together with avant-garde artists and writers. Starting in 1923, he solicited the collaboration of a number of Constructivist designers including Aleksei Levin, Aleksandr Rodchenko, and Vavara Stepanova, to produce advertising and literacy posters for state agencies. Throughout the 1920s, Maiakovskii continued to work as a poet and writer. His publications were often designed by artists such as El Lissitzky and Rodchenko. In 1930, Maiakovskii committed suicide.

IVAN MALIUTIN (1889–1932)

Before the Revolution, Maliutin worked primarily designing theatrical costumes. After the Revolution, he exhibited with the Knave of Diamonds group in Moscow in 1917, and at the Fifth State Exhibition in 1918–19. In 1919, he joined the Moscow ROSTA poster-making collaborative and produced hundreds of poster series. Throughout the twenties he contributed to satirical journals such as *Krokodil* [Crocodile], *Bezbozhnik* [Atheist], and *Begemot* [Hippopotamus].

DMITRII STAKHIEVICH MOOR (1883–1946)

Moor was born in Novocherkassk with the name of Orlov. He was schooled in Kiev, Kharkov, and Moscow. In 1906 he helped to set up an underground print shop with equipment smuggled from the shop where he was employed, where he published his first satirical cartoons. Between 1908 and 1917, his cartoons were accepted at several satirical journals including *Kimval* [Cymbal], *Utro vechera mudrenee* [Sleep On It], *Satirikon*, and *Budil'nik* [Alarm Clock]. During this time his signature changed from Dor, to Mor, and finally to Moor. In 1914, with Russia's entrance into World War I, he produced patriotic works in the style of *lubki*, the vernacular Russian print form. By 1916 he was serving as one of the editors of *Budil'nik*. After the October Revolution, Moor continued to produce newspaper graphics and also began to create political posters. During the Civil War years he produced about fifty of these latter, the majority for Revvoensovet [the Revolutionary-Military Council of the Republic]. He also participated in decorating Moscow for festival celebrations and for a short while probably worked in the Moscow ROSTA collaborative. In 1922 he co-founded the satirical magazine *Krokodil* [Crocodile], and he illustrated anti-religious books and journals such as *Bezbozhnik* [Atheist]. He taught at the VKhUTEMAS from 1922 to 1930. His work was represented in the Exposition international des arts décoratifs et industriels modernes in Paris in 1925 and in the Seventh Exhibition of *L'Araignee* [The Spider] at Galerie Devambe in Paris the same year. His work was also included in an exhibition of revolutionary posters in Berlin in 1927 and in the Exhibition of Graphic Arts, Poster, and Book Design in Danzig in 1930. In 1928, Moor join the *Oktiabr'* [October] group as a founding member, and exhibited with them in 1930. He contributed satirical drawings to the magazine *Daesh'*, largely a collaboration of members of the *Oktiabr'* group, in 1929. In addition to poster design and satirical cartoons, Moor created theatrical designs and book illustrations. He was named an Honored Art Worker of the Russian Federation and was elected to the presidium of the Union of Revolutionary Poster Workers in 1931. Moor was also elected to a political position in the Moscow City Soviet in 1935.

NATAL'IA PINUS

A pupil of Gustav Klutsis, Pinus was a member of the *Oktiabr'* [October] group, and exhibited with them in Gorkii Park in Moscow, 1931. In the fall of that year, after extensive criticism of *Oktiabr'*, Pinus (along with Klutsis, Valentina Kulagina, and Sergei Sen'kin) disassociated herself from the group and requested permission to join RAPKh [the Russian Association of Proletarian Artists].

ALEKSEI ALEKSANDROVICH RADAKOV (1879–1942)

Radakov was born in Moscow, the son of a doctor. He studied at the Stieglitz School in St. Petersburg, then at Moscow College in the School of Painting, Sculpture, and Architecture. Before the Revolution, Radakov worked as a theater organizer, set designer, and art teacher. He also contributed satirical drawings to the journals *Noyvi Satirikon* and *Galochonok*. After the Revolution, Radakov designed decorations for revolutionary festivals in 1918 and continued to produce caricatures, theater designs, journals, and posters. He directed the art section of the children's department of Gosizdat [the State Publishing House] in Petrograd. Radakov created works for the Moscow ROSTA collaborative and contributed occasionally to the work of the Petrograd ROSTA group. His work was included at the 1922 Exhibition of the Book in Florence, the Exposition international des arts décoratifs et industriels modernes in Paris in 1925, and the Seventh Exhibition of *L'Araignee* [The Spider] at the Galerie Devambe in Paris the same year. From 1922 to 1929 he contributed to satirical journals such as *Lapot'* [Straw Shoe], *Begemot*

[Hippopotamus], *Bezbozhnik* [Atheist], and *Krokodil* [Crocodile]. He was a founding member of the Society of Soviet Artists in 1929. After 1941, Radakov was involved in the production of the World War II revival of ROSTA windows, called "Tass Windows."

ALEKSANDR MIKHAILOVICH RODCHENKO (1891–1956)

In 1911, Rodchenko began his studies at the Kazan Art School. There he met Vavara Stepanova, whom he later married. In 1914, he moved to Moscow and began to study sculpture and architecture at the Stroganov Institute. Rodchenko participated in Vladimir Tatlin's 1916 exhibition, The Store. In 1917 he helped found the Union of Painters, a organization representing a broad spectrum of artists; Rodchenko became the secretary of its avant-garde section and was given a solo exhibition by the group. That year he also collaborated on the design of elements of the Café Pittoresque. From 1918 to 1922 he was actively involved in IZO Narkompros [the Department of Fine Art of the Commissariat of Enlightenment], and became the head of the Museum Bureau and the Director of the Museum of Painterly Culture, supervising the acquisition of hundreds of contemporary works for the state. From 1918 to 1921, he made a series of spatial constructions. In 1921, at the exhibition 5x5=25, Rodchenko exhibited a monochrome triptych "Red, Yellow and Blue" along with two complementary works, "Line" and "Cell," and thereafter abandoned painting. Rodchenko joined the INKhUK [Institute of Artistic Culture] in 1920 and became the head of the First Working Group of Constructivists. From 1920 to 1930 Rodchenko served on the faculty of VKhUTEMAS [Higher State Artistic and Technical Workshops], which became VKhUTEIN [Higher State Artistic and Technical Institute] in 1927–28. In 1923, he created a series of photomontages to accompany Vladimir Maiakovskii's poem "*Pro Eto*" [About This]. From 1923 on, he worked in graphic design, often collaborating with Maiakovskii on advertisements and posters for state agencies. Around 1924 he began taking photographs. Rodchenko designed a model workers' club for the 1925 Exposition international des arts décoratifs et industriels modernes in Paris and traveled to Paris to oversee its execution. He designed the sets for several films and theatrical productions including the second part of "The Bedbug," by Maiakovskii at the Meyerhold Theater in 1929. From 1928 to 1932 he produced photographic essays on industrial subjects. In 1931, he traveled on assignment to the construction site of the White Sea Canal, built by prison labor, and from the photographs taken, he designed a photo-story for the magazine *SSR na stroike* [USSR in Construction]. In the mid-thirties, he returned to painting.

VLADIMIR O. ROSKIN (1896–1929)

Roskin studied at the Stroganov Institute from 1910 to 1913. After the Revolution, he joined the Moscow ROSTA collaborative. He exhibited at the Fifth State Exhibition in Moscow in 1918–19, and appeared on a list in April 1919 of artists whose works were approved for acquisition by the Museum of Painterly Culture. From 1924 on, he designed Soviet exhibitions abroad including the Pressa exhibition in Cologne, Germany in 1928, on which he collaborated with El Lissitzky and others.

ALEKSANDR NIKOLAEVICH SAMOKHVALOV (1894–1971)

Samokhvalov studied at the Higher Art School at the Academy of Arts in St. Petersburg from 1914 to 1917, and the Petrograd SVOMAS [the State Free Art Workshops] and VKhUTEMAS [Higher State Artistic and Technical Workshops] from 1920 to 1923. Besides painting, Samokhvalov worked as a poster artist and created decorations for mass festivals. He exhibited with the World of Art group in 1917, with the Circle of Artists from 1927 to 1929, and with the *Oktiabr'* [October] group in 1930. Samokhvalov's work was included in the 1923 survey, Exhibition of Paintings by Petrograd Artists of All Tendencies, 1919–1923, the Exposition internationale des arts décoratifs et industriels modernes in Paris in 1925, and an exhibition of acquisitions for the State Art Collection in 1928. He was represented in the 1932 jubilee exhibition of Artists of the RSFSR at the Russian Museum in Leningrad. He taught monumental painting in Leningrad from 1948 to 1951.

ELENA SEMENOVA (1898–?)

Semenova entered the Sculpture Faculty of the SVOMAS [Second State Free Art Studios in Moscow] in 1919. In 1922, she transferred to the architecture section of VKhUTEMAS, but left in 1924 without graduating. In the mid-twenties she produced designs for small-scale architectural structures, interiors, and display units; from the late twenties to early thirties, she focused on graphic design. She contributed to the Constructivist journals *Lef* [Left (1923–25)] and *Novyi lef* [New Left (1927–28)]. In 1927 she was invited along with Vavara Stepanova and E. Lavinskaia to submit designs for the decoration of several squares in Moscow and to design posters to mark the tenth anniversary of the Revolution. Semenova collaborated with Lavinskaia on the design of window displays for Dom Knigi, the state bookstore. From the 1930s on, she worked primarily as a designer for exhibitions and trade shows.

SERGEI YAKOVLEVICH SEN'KIN (1894–1963)

Sen'kin's artistic training began at the Moscow School of Painting, Sculpture, and Architecture, which he attended from 1914 until 1915. He studied from 1918 to 1919 in Kazimir Malevich's studio at SVOMAS [the Second State Free Art Workshops in Moscow], later maintaining contact with Malevich at Vitebsk. He apparently worked as an army artist in the Urals during 1920. The following year he reassumed his full-time artistic education at the Moscow VKhUTEMAS [Higher State Artistic and Technical Workshops]. According to one of the UNOVIS [Affirmers of the New Art] journals, Sen'kin and Gustav Klutsis cooperatively set up an independent studio at the VKhUTEMAS, where Klutsis's paintings and Sen'kin's analyses of form-making typified the "new practical realism" of UNOVIS. In 1921 Sen'kin displayed his work in the VKhUTEMAS students' Cézanne Club's exhibition, and in 1922 he exhibited Suprematist works at the Association of New Trends in Art in Petrograd. In 1924 he and Klutsis established the Workshop of the Revolution within VKhUTEMAS, which stressed the development of an artistic practice geared toward the masses and collective revolutionary aims. Sen'kin was associated with the Constructivist journal *Lef* [Left (1923–25)]. He joined the *Oktiabr'* [October] group in 1928 and in the same year collaborated with El Lissitzky on the photomontage display for the Soviet Pavilion at the Pressa exhibition in Cologne. He participated in the Exposition of the *Oktiabr'* group in Moscow in 1930 and the Photomontage exhibition in Berlin in 1931. Also in 1931, he joined RAPKh [the Russian Association of Proletarian Artists]. Although his work in the 1920s was primarily photomontage—some of which he contributed to the journal *SSR na stroike* [USSR in Construction]—he also designed mass festival decorations, posters, books, and magazines.

GEORGII AVGUSTOVICH STENBERG (1900–1933)
VLADIMIR AVGUSTOVICH STENBERG (1899–1982)

The Stenberg brothers, sons of a Russian mother and a Swedish father (who returned to Sweden in 1921), were born in Moscow and retained Swedish citizenship. Encouraged by their father, a painter, the brothers studied enamel and ceramic decorations and stage design from 1912 to 1917 at the Stroganov Art School, which merged with the Institute of Fine Arts in 1918 to become SVOMAS [State Free Art Atudios]. There the Stenbergs studied with Georgii Yakulov. They also, in 1917, took a course in military engineering, concentrating on railroad construction and bridge design. For May Day and the October Revolution anniversary celebration the following year, they helped create urban agit-decorations for the Post Office on Miasnitskaia Street, and by themselves they decorated the Napoleon Cinema and the Railway Workers' Club. In 1919 the Stenbergs helped found OBMOKhU [the Association of Young Artists], exhibiting four times with the group in 1919, 1920, 1921, and 1923. As members of INKhUK [Institute of Artistic Culture], they associated themselves with the First Working Group of Constructivists and took part in its discussions in 1920 and 1921. In January 1922, together with Konstantin Medunetskii, they exhibited their spatial paintings and non-objective constructions at the Kafe Poetov in Moscow, publishing the first declarations of the principles of Constructivism in the accompanying catalog, entitled *The Constructivists*. The Stenbergs exhibited thirty-two works made from metal, glass, and wood, which they considered models for new types of buildings. Together with Medunetskii they delivered a paper on February 4, 1922 to INKhUK, elaborating the foundations of their approach. As part of a group of artists including Aleksei Gan, Aleksandr Rodchenko, and Vavara Stepanova, they rejected "pure art" and joined in support of an artistic practice linked to industry. They participated in 1922 in the First Exhibition of Russian Art in Berlin. Between 1922 and 1931 the Stenbergs created the sets and costumes for Alexander Tairov's Kamernyi [Chamber]

Theater and for the Moscow Music Hall. Touring with Tairov's theater in 1923 they visited Paris, where they exhibited their work and met Pablo Picasso, whose neo-classical canvases disappointed them. Together with Aleksandra Ekster and Ignati Nivinskii they worked on the decorations of pavilions at the 1923 agricultural exhibition. From 1928 on, the Stenbergs were in charge of the celebration decorations for Red Square in Moscow. From the early 1920s, they constructed architectural designs, produced agit-posters during the civil war, and made over 300 film posters for Goskino (the State cinema). They also produced many photomontages and book and magazine covers. Between 1923 and 1925, they were closely connected with the constructivist magazine *Lef* [Left]. The Stenbergs were awarded a Gold Medal for stage design at the 1925 Exposition international des arts décoratifs et industriels modernes in Paris. They helped organize exhibitions of film posters in 1925 and 1927, and they took part in the Film und Foto exhibition in Stuttgart in 1929 and in the Photomontage exhibition in Berlin in 1931.

Georgii Stenberg designed interiors for the Palace of Culture in Leninskaia Sloboda, and was chief artist for the Gor'kii Park of Culture and Leisure in Moscow. In 1933, he died in a car accident. Vladimir Stenberg continued to design poster and street decorations, and until 1948, he participated in the decoration of Red Square for the anniversary of the Revolution. In 1933, he became a Soviet citizen. Arrested in 1952 during one of Stalin's purges, he was freed and rehabilitated after Stalin's death.

VAVARA STEPANOVA (1894–1958)

Stepanova was born in Kovno (now Kaunas), Lithuania. She studied at the Kazan Art School from 1910 to 1913, where she met Aleksandr Rodchenko, whom she later married. She moved to Moscow in 1915, where she studied with the impressionists Kostantin Yuon and Il'ia Mashkov. After the Revolution, Stepanova became deputy head of the literary-artistic section of IZO Narkompros [the Department of Fine Art of the Commissariat of Enlightenment]. From 1918 on she contributed to many exhibitions, including the Fifth, Tenth, and Nineteenth State Exhibitions, the 5x5=25 exhibition in 1921, the First Russian Art Exhibition in Berlin in 1922, and the Exposition international des arts décoratifs et industriels modernes in Paris in 1925. From 1920 to 1923, she was a member of INKhUK [Institute of Artistic Culture] and associated herself first with the Objective Analysis Group and then with the First Working Group of Constructivists. In 1921, she delivered an important lecture, "Constructivism," which served as a focus for debate at INKhUK. She was associated with the Constructivist magazines *Lef* [Left (1923–25)] and *Novyi lef* [New Left (1927–28)]. She created the designs for the set of "Death of Tarelkin" at the Meyerhold Theater in 1922. She began to concentrate on the design of magazines, books, and posters in the mid-twenties. From 1920 to 1925 Stepanova taught art at the Academy of Social Education, and from 1924 to 1925 she was a professor in the textile faculty at VKhUTEMAS [Higher State Artistic and Technical Workshops]. In 1945, Stepanova became art director for the magazine *Sovetskaia Zhenshchina* [Soviet Woman].

WLADYSLAW STRZEMINSKI (VLADISLAV STRZHEMINSKII) (1893–1952)

After recovering from a serious injury inflicted in World War I, Strzeminski studied at the Moscow SVOMAS [the State Free Art Workshops] from 1918 to 1919. In 1919, he worked for the Central Bureau of Exhibitions within IZO Narkompros [the Department of Fine Art of the Commissariat of Enlightenment] and then with the Moscow Art Board, which oversaw the activities of IZO Narkompros in that city. In 1920, he married Katarzyna Kobro, a sculptor closely associated with the Constructivists. Together they moved to Vitebsk, where they were attracted by Kazimir Malevich's Suprematism and became members of UNOVIS [Affirmers of the New Art]. With Kobro, Strzeminski moved to Smolensk, where he taught at the Free Art Workshops and was involved in the local branch of UNOVIS; he appears to have directed the poster-making activities of the Russian Telegraph Agency [ROSTA] in Smolensk. Strzeminski went to Poland in 1922, and Kobro joined him there in 1924. Together they founded the School for Modern Typography in Lodz in 1931. Strzeminski continued to paint, defining a mode of abstraction called "unism," which was much influenced by Malevich's Suprematism.

ADOF IOSIPOVICH STRAKHOV(-BRASLAVSKII) (1896–1979)

Strakhov-Braslavskii was born at Ekaterinoslav in the Ukraine and graduated from the Odessa Art School in 1915. During the first Soviet years, he designed posters, made sketches for revolutionary celebration decorations, and contributed illustrations to magazines. His work was represented in the Exposition international des arts décoratifs et industriels modernes in Paris in 1925 and the Exhibition of Revolutionary Posters in Berlin in 1927. Later he worked mainly in sculpture and poster design and was named People's Artist of the Ukrainian Soviet Socialist Republic in 1944.

BORIS TITOV

Although his work was much influenced by the Constructivists, Titov was associated with AKhRR [Association of Artists of Revolutionary Russia], a group who called for a new proletarian art based on the models of nineteenth-century realism.

NIKOLAI STEPANOVICH TROSHIN (1897–?)

Troshin studied at the Penza School of Art and then, in 1922, at the VKhUTEMAS [Higher Sate Artistic and Technical Workshops] in Moscow. He was active in the 1920s and 30s as a poster designer, an illustrator of books, and as an exhibition designer.

Artist's biographies by T.J. Demos and Stephanie Tayengco

SELECT BIBLIOGRAPHY

The Aesthetic Arsenal: Socialist Realism Under Stalin. NY: The Institute for
    Contemporary Art, P.S. 1 Museum, 1993.

Anikst, Mikhail, ed. *Soviet Commercial Design of the Twenties*. Catherine Cooke, trans.
    London: Thames and Hudson, 1987.

Arwas, Victor, ed. "The Great Russian Utopia." *Art and Design Profile* no. 29
    (London: 1993).

Bailes, Kendall, E. *Technology and Society under Lenin and Stalin: Origins of the
    Soviet Technical Intelligentsia, 1917–1941*. Princeton: Princeton University
    Press, 1978.

Barkhatova, Elena, ed. *Russian Constructivist Posters*. Moscow/Paris: Avantgarde, 1992.

Bois, Yve-Alain. "El Lissitzky: Radical Reversibility," *Art in America* vol. 76, no. 4
    (April 1988): 161–180.

Bojko, Szymon. *New Graphic Design in Revolutionary Russia*. New York: Praeger
    Publishers, 1972.

Bonnell, Victoria, E. "The Peasant Woman in Stalinist Political Art of the 1930s,"
    American Historical Review vol. 98, no. 1 (February 1993): 55–82.

Bowlt, John, ed. and trans. *Russian Art of the Avant-Garde: Theory and Criticism*,
    2nd ed. New York: Thames and Hudson, 1988.

Buchloh, Benjamin H.D. "From Faktura to Factography," *October* 30 (Fall 1984).
    Reprinted in Annette Michelson et al., eds., *October: The First Decade*.
    Cambridge: MIT Press, 1987, 77–112.

B. S. Butnik-Siverskii. *Sovetskii plakat epokhi grazhdanskoi voiny, 1918–1921*.
    Moscow: Izdatel'stvo vsesoiuznoi knizhnoi palaty, 1960.

Constantine, Mildred and Alan Fern. *Revolutionary Soviet Film Posters*.
    Baltimore: The Johns Hopkins University Press, 1974.

Duvakin, Viktor. "Okna ROSTA i Glavpolitprosveta," in Vladimir Maiakovskii,
    Polnoe sobranie sochinenii. Vol. 3. Moscow: Khudozhestvennaia literatura,
    1957, 469–480.

Fitzpatrick, Sheila. *The Russian Revolution*. 2nd. ed. Oxford: Oxford University
    Press, 1994.

——, ed. *Cultural Revolution in Russia, 1928–1931*. Bloomington: Indiana
    University Press, 1978.

——, Alexander Rabinowitch, and Richard Stites, eds. *Russia in the Era of NEP:
    Explorations in Soviet Society and Culture*. Bloomington: Indiana University
    Press, 1991.

Galerie Gmurzynska, *From Painting to Design. Russian Constructivist Art of the
    Twenties*. Cologne: Galerie Gmurzynska, 1981.

Gassner, Hubertus. "Heartfield's Moscow Apprenticeship," in Peter Pachnicke and
    Klaus Honnef, eds., *John Heartfield*. New York: Abrams, 1992.

—— and Eckhart Gillen, eds. *Zwischen Revolutionkunst und
    Sozialistischen Realismus: Dokumente und Kommentare
    Kunstdebatten in der Sowjetunion von 1917 bis 1934*. Cologne: DuMont
    Buchverlag, 1979.

—— and Roland Nachtigiller, eds. *Gustav Klutsis: Retrospektive*. Stuttgart:
    Verlag Gerd Hatje, 1991.

Golomstock, Igor. *Totalitarian Art in the Soviet Union, the Third Reich, Fascist
    Italy, and the People's Republic of China*. Robert Chandler, trans.
    London: Collins Harvill, 1990.

The Guggenheim Museum. *The Great Utopia: The Russian and Soviet Avant-Garde,
    1915–1932*. In association with exhibition held 25 September–
    15 December 1992. New York: Solomon R. Guggenheim Museum, 1992.

Gunther, Hans, ed. *The Culture of the Stalin Period*. New York: St. Martin's Press in
    association with the School of Slavonic and East European Studies,
    University of London, 1990.

Henry Art Gallery. *Art into Life: Russian Constructivism, 1914–1932*.
    Seattle: Henry Art Gallery; New York: Rizzoli, 1990.

Kenez, Peter. *The Birth of the Propaganda State: Soviet Methods of Mass
    Mobilization, 1917–1929*. Cambridge: Cambridge University Press, 1985.

Kunst und Propaganda: Sowjetische Plakate bis 1953. Catalog for exhibition at
    Museum für Gestaltung Zurich, 1 June–13 August 1989.

Leclanche-Boulé, Claude. *Le Constructivisme Russe: Typographies and Photomontages*. Paris: Flammarion, 1991.

Liakov, V. *Sovetskii reklamnyi plakat, 1917–32*. Moscow: Sovetskii khudozhnik, 1970.

Lodder, Christina. *Russian Constructivism*. New Haven: Yale University Press, 1983.

Matsa, I. et al. *Sovetskoe iskusstvo za 15 let: Materialy i dokumentatsiia*. Moscow-Leningrad: Ogiz-Izogiz, 1933.

Milner, John, ed. *A Dictionary of Russian and Soviet Artists, 1420–1970*. Woodbridge, Suffolk: Antique Collectors' Club, 1993.

Noever, Peter, ed. *Aleksandr M. Rodchenko-Vavara F. Stepanova: The Future is Our Only Goal*. Munich: Prestel Verlag, 1991.

Oginskaia, Larisa. *Gustav Klutsis*. Moscow: Sovetskii Khudozhnik, 1981.

Paret, Peter, Beth Irwin Lewis, and Paul Paret. *Persuasive Images: Posters of War and Revolution from the Hoover Institution Archives*. Princeton: Princeton University Press, 1992.

Polonskii, Viacheslav. *Russkii revoliutsionnyi plakat*. Moscow: Gosizdat, 1925.

Rosenberg, William G. and Lewis H. Siegelbaum, eds. *Social Dimensions of Soviet Industrialization*. Bloomington: Indiana University Press, 1993.

Sander Gallery. *ROSTA: Bolshevik Placards, 1919–1921. Handmade Political Posters from the Russian Telegraph Agency*. New York: Sander Gallery, 1994.

Sotheby's. *USSR in Construction: Posters, Designs and Drawings*. Catalog of a sale held in New York on 10 March 1994.

Stites, Richard. *Revolutionary Dreams: Utopian Vision and Experimental Life in the Russian Revolution*. New York and Oxford: Oxford University Press, 1989.

Suvorova, K.N. et al. *V.V. Maiakovskii. Opisanie dokumental'nykh materialov: "Okna" ROSTA i Glavpolitprosveta, 1919–22*. Moscow: TsGALI, 1964.

Taylor, Brandon. *Art and Literature Under the Bolsheviks. Volume 1: The Crisis of Renewal, 1917–1924*. London and Concord: Pluto Press, 1991.

——. *Art and Literature under the Bolsheviks. Volume 2: Authority and Revolution, 1924–1932*. London: Pluto Press, 1992.

Tradition and Revolution. Catalog to accompany *Leningrad in Manchester* exhibitions, 16 June–22 July 1990. Manchester: Cornerhouse Publications in association with the Olympic Festival, 1990.

Tupitsyn, Margarita. "From the Politics of Montage to the Montage of Politics: Soviet Practice 1919 through 1937," in Matthew Teitelbaum, ed., *Montage and Modern Life, 1919–1942*. Boston: The Institute of Contemporary Art and Cambridge: MIT Press, 1992.

——. "Gustav Klutsis: Between Art and Politics," *Art in America* vol. 79, no. 1 (1991): 41–47.

White, Stephen. *The Bolshevik Poster*. New Haven: Yale University Press, 1988.

Wood, Paul. "Realisms and Realities," in Briony Fer, David Batchelor, and Paul Wood, *Realism, Rationalism, Surrealism: Art Between the Wars*. New Haven: Yale University Press in association with The Open University, 1993.

ACKNOWLEDGEMENTS

The exhibition and catalog could not have been produced without the assistance and support of many people. Eleanor Barefoot introduced me to Merrill Berman and helped formulate the initial idea for the show. Johanna Drucker offered both her encouragement and criticism in timely doses. Ellen Lupton thought a full-color catalog was a good idea and proposed the idea to Princeton Architectural Press, and Kevin Lippert agreed to take on the project. Jim Frank produced wonderful color transparencies, and helped gather all kinds of information about specific posters. Allison Saltzman made sense of the chaos of images and texts I presented her. Susan Brook helped me with the translations of the poster texts, and Hilde Hoogenboom refined them. Maria Gough helped me clarify my thinking about the exhibition and the catalog over many conversations, and she contributed an important essay to the catalog. Juliet Koss edited both my essay and the selection of works for the show. Richard Meyer read an earlier version of my essay and offered many useful suggestions. Michael Cader, Elaine Koss, Peter Galassi, and Mary Dickerman all provided advice at key moments. At the Wallach Art Gallery, Sally Weiner, Liz Bigham, Jonathan Munk, Amy Schlegel, Toni Simon, and Frances Yuan wore many hats in providing the administrative and organizational support the exhibition required. Friends in the Department of Art

History at Columbia University—Joan Cummins, Jonathan Gilmore, Cathryn Steeves, and Paul Sternberger—vetted works over lunch with good humor. My family and Jean-Christophe Castelli helped and encouraged me in many ways. Fellowships from the Center for Advanced Studies in the Visual Arts at the National Gallery in Washington, D.C. supported both Maria Gough and me during the time in which the exhibition and catalog were prepared. I am, in addition, most grateful to two anonymous donors, who made the exhibition possible, and to Merrill Berman.

Leah Dickerman